Victoria
ISN'T THE ONLY
Sister WITH A
SECRET

Victoria isn't the Only *Sister* with a **SECRET**

ARLICIA ALBERT

Victoria Isn't the Only Sister with a Secret
by Arlicia Albert

Cover Design by Alfred Beverly II, CEO of Charis Solutions
Photography (www.charis-solutionsphotography.com)

© Copyright 2015

SAINT PAUL PRESS, DALLAS, TEXAS

First Printing, 2015

All scripture quotations, unless otherwise listed, are taken from the Thompson Chain Reference Study Bible (King James Version).

ISBN-10: 0-9963241-7-8
ISBN-13: 978-0-9963241-7-5

Printed in the U.S.A.

Contents

Acknowledgments
& Dedications

First and foremost, Lord, I thank you for entrusting me with your miracle! Thank you Lord for allowing my life to be a true testament of your power, your mercy, and your grace.

I do not have the right words to express the love and appreciation I have for the people that helped to put this manuscript to print. I began writing this book prior to suffering my ruptured brain aneurysm and due to my memory loss and other health challenges I did not think my dream would ever come true, BUT God.

Lord thank you for loving me so much that you have strategically placed an army of people in my life that would pray Reinhold Niebuhr's prayer of courage with me:

"God grant me the serenity to accept the things I cannot change, the courage to change the things I can, and the wisdom to know the difference."

My life may not be going the way I planned it, but it is going EXACTLY the way God planned it.

To my husband, Wendell "Reese" Albert:

Thank you for being my everything! You are the reason for the smile on my face, the swing in my step, the sway in my hips, and the glide in my stride! You are a wonderful husband, an AWESOME provider, a loving father, a faithful friend, and my biggest cheerleader.

To my daughters, Lyndsey & Wendy:

You are definitely the wind beneath my wings!

Honestly, you are the FIGHT that's inside of me. Your faces light a fire inside of me that I can't even begin to explain. All I have ever wanted to do is make you proud to tell the world, "That's my mama!"

To my son, Joshua Albert:

Thank you for embracing me with your love and accepting me into your life. I am so proud of you and the man you have become. You are walking in the favor of God and every step you take I can see Psalm 37:23 unfolding in your life. You are an AMAZING young man and the Lord is leading and guiding your journey!

To my parents, Alfred & Audrey Beverly Sr.

Thank you for being my rock! Mom & Dad you are my strength and I thank God for the foundation you laid for our family. Thank you for your love, your faith, and for living the life you preach about. Thank you for spending all of your life investing in my future.

This book is the fruit of your labor. It is my prayer that I have made you proud.

To my siblings: Arnita (Nee-Nee) Williams & Alfred (Brother) Beverly II

Thank you for always supporting me in every part of my life. I don't know where I would be without your consistent love and faithfulness. Nee you are a rare jewel and every part of my life shines brighter because you are in it! Brother - Charis Solutions Photography, you have a craft that captures the beauty of life. Your gift is definitely grace given. Thank you for always bringing my visions to life!

To my Pastor & Friend Dr. John R. Adolph

Thank you for your consistent Godly example! You have been a positive influence in every aspect of my life and I am forever grateful. You have pushed me, prepared me and propelled me as a preacher, teacher, and a writer. Thank you for teaching me "EVERYTHING" I know about ministry. You are ABSOLUTELY the most dynamic Pastor/Preacher on the earth. I know without a shadow of doubt that I am Following Favored Feet!

To my Executive Assistant, Karen Spears

Thank you for your labor, loyalty, and love. You work to make my life easier and you have no idea what that means to me. There is no way that I can do the things that I have been called to do without having you in my life. Kay-Kay you have a heart made of gold and the patience of Job. Thank you for always believing in me.

Hugs & Kisses to the best of the best!!!

My Editorial Advisory Board

Dr. John R. Adolph   Dr. Natalie Francisco
Dr. Porchanee' White
Mollyn Cole   Arnita Williams

Thank you guys for propelling me into my purpose. I appreciate the tireless hours each of you spent editing my work and God knows

I really appreciate your patience.

Thank you for the "You Can Do This" speeches each one of you spoke into my life just when I needed them most.

I Will ALWAYS Love You!

MYE320 Board Members

Wendell Albert   Zandra Collins

Justin Henderson

Christy Staples   Karen Spears

Arnita Williams

Thank you guys for sowing your gifts and talents into MYE320!

I appreciate you and Thank God for you daily.

Without you in my life my dreams and visions would never materialize!

Thank you for supporting me and encouraging me!

You are my Dream Team!

My Treasure Chest

Every woman should have a special place to store her most prized possessions. A place dedicated to house things of value and worth.

My Treasure Chest is filled with the women in my life that contribute to three of my most essential values: My Past, My Present, & My Future.

My life has been made the better because of the treasures I have found in each of you.

~ My Past ~

In loving memory of my grandfather, Mr. Lucius Goudeau Sr. and my aunt, Mrs. Mae Ceola Williams; both of their lives ended as the result of ruptured brain aneurysms.

And to my God-Mother, Mrs. Mobile Beverly, who lost her fight to breast cancer. Nanny Mobile, thank you for introducing me to Reese. You were right, he is the man for me!

~ My Present ~
My Mother - Mrs. Audrey Ray Beverly
My Grandmother - Mrs. Willie Mae Goudeau
My Aunts - Ms. Virginia Joseph, Ms. Antoinette Goudeau
& Mrs. Alnetta Goudeau-Baker
My Cousins -
Mrs. Cheryl Hammond   Ms. Dionne Thompson
Ms. Raina Curry
My Role Model - Mrs. Delores Darby
My Little Sister - Mrs. Arnita Williams

My Sisters-In-Law

Ms. Brizet Albert   Mrs. Kimberly Albert

Mrs. Starla Beverly

My Daughter-In-Law
Mrs. Jailand Albert

My Grandson
Jaxon M. Albert

My Sister Friends

Dorrie Adolph   Yolanda Carroll

Natalie Francisco   Jillander Sturges

Mia Wright   Felicia Young

My Brain Aneurysm Survivor Sisters

Leslie Lindsay   Iwona Kmbacka   Peggie Plosa

Mrs. OJ Proske   Robin Reid   Anita Rosales

Janet Saxon   Lisa Sonka   Carmen Speets

Janet Sutherland   Colleen Teears

My Brain Aneurysm Survivor Brothers

Michael Vann Deloatch Jr.   Tony Hill

~ My Future ~

The words from the lips of an 18-year-old young lady changed my life forever. I had just finished preaching and was asked to greet the congregation at the rear of the church. This beautiful young lady walked up to me and asked for a hug and to take a picture with me. She then asked if she could have my autograph. I smiled thinking WOW why in the world would she want my autograph. I said okay and signed her church bulletin. As I continued to greet people, I noticed the young lady was still standing around. As we proceeded back to the Pastor's Study, I walked over to her and gave her another hug, and she said, "Minister Albert, you have changed my life forever!" Those six words have been etched in my spirit and changed how I see myself, who I am, and what I do.

"You Have Changed My Life Forever!"

My Treasure Chest is filled with the precious jewels listed below. I pray daily that my life is an example to these AMAZING you women and encourages these future leaders to live on purpose, fulfill their purpose and leave a rich legacy to those following their footsteps.

My Daughters

Lyndsey Michelle Barton-Albert
& Wendy Nichelle Albert

My Nieces

Kierra Albert   Amiyah Beverly

Kristina Addison Johnson

Courtney Williams   Tajah Williams

Vintrice Albert-Wright

My God-Daughters

Sumone Adolph   Renea James

Arianna Sturges   Brianna Sturges-Johns

Addison-Grace Johns   Mai'Zhrae Zeno

My God-Sons

Jonathan R. Adolph   Alfred J. Beverly III

Justin Henderson

My Precious Jewels

April Alfred   Bria Baldwin   Devyn Baldwin

Daisha Bennett   Victoria Brown

Erika Claiborne   Elesha Collins

Charleigh Clayton   Chelsea Clayton

Adaja Copes   Denaja Copes   Teja Copes

Diandra Darby   Deandra Darby   Layna Lewis

Candace Lewis   Tarah Lewis-Armstrong

Mylerra Lewis   Candise Henderson

Jamesha Flakes-Berry   Brittany Hayes

Jzmynee Flakes   Johnetta Williams-Boykins

Lauren Francisco   Lesley Francisco-McClendon

Nicole Francisco-Bailey   Candace Goldman

Eva Goldman   Precious Goldman-Bob

Isean Isedore   LaErica Isedore   Maiya Williams

Tajah Shipp   Alexia Jones   Jasmyne Johnson

Jelisa Johnson   Ashley Joseph   Joyce Kennerson

Bryanna Lewis   Jeanique Newton

Renata Rawlins   Ebony Strange

Nadria Robinson   Dayla Sanders

Amanda Spears   Carla Spears-Pitre

Morgan Thompson   Mia Thompson

Riz Washington   Brooklyn Williams

Clarissa Willliams   Montia Williams

Foreword
by Dr. John R. Adolph

Hidden human secrets often reveal the flaws and failures of people. Secrets often contain the mistakes of men, the misques of women, the mystery of life's uncertainties, the mishaps of human error and the misfortunes of poor choices that yield negative returns on some of life's greatest investments. In her provocative new book, *Victoria Isn't the Only Sister With a Secret*, Arlicia Albert grabs these SECRETS by the collar like a woman who is fed up with the damage they can cause and brings them to the cross of Jesus Christ for the purpose of healing, deliverance and redemption.

I have had the paramount pleasure of working with Arlicia for nearly twenty years in a Kingdom Building capacity at the Antioch Church of Beaumont, Texas. She has a passion for excellence that drives me and this text is her greatest work thus far! With the wit of a sister, the calling of a preacher, the doctrinal teaching of a systematic theologian and the skill of a play write from Hollywood this book gets to the core of human depravity and heals each reader through the Lord's evidenced love for us expressed at calvary.

This book is a must read! After all, *Victoria Isn't the Only Sister With a Secret*. You have some secrets too. But after reading this text, you will celebrate the healing and forgiveness found in the person of Jesus Christ, Son of the living God!

Dr. John R. Adolph, Pastor
Antioch Missionary Baptist Church
Beaumont, Texas

Foreword

by Dr. Natalie A. Francisco

I am both delighted and excited to commend to you this first of many books to be written by my sister and best friend, Arlicia R. Albert. *Victoria Isn't the Only Sister with a Secret,* is a captivating story of a woman whose life travels down a treacherous road of unexpected twists and turns that leaves her feeling helpless and hopeless. There are many women who, although their issues may be different, will be drawn into the life of Victoria and the other characters in this fictitious story in ways that are surprising, entertaining and intriguing. In fact, reading this book is like sitting in a theatre and watching the production of the story line play out on the screen of your mind.

Arlicia's creativity and wit, as well as her uncanny way of relating to women of all ages and backgrounds, remind us that God is able to take the ashes of our past, no matter how shameful and secretive, and replace it with beauty and a renewed sense of belonging that reaffirms our original virtue and value.

Thank you, Arlicia, for sharing one of your many gifts with the world by writing and releasing this book. Even more so, thank you for the miraculous manifestation of your life as a woman who has survived and thrived despite the odds that were set against you. God spared your life, saved you from a rare brain aneurysm, and is using your many gifts to impact the world in ways that only you can...but that's another story. I am so proud of the woman you are and the multitudes of people whose lives will be transformed by your obedience to follow God's lead. You, my dear friend, are a phenomenal woman whose time to shine brilliantly has come. May God's light emanating from you penetrate the dark, secretive hearts of those who long to discover freedom from guilt, shame and condemnation so that they can live in victory.

Dr. Natalie A. Francisco
Founder/Executive Director,
Women of Worth & Worship (WOWW), LLC
Speaker, Pastor, Author & Mentor
Calvary Community Church (C3)
Hampton, VA & Atlanta, GA
www.C3Hampton.org / www.C3Atlanta.org
www.NatalieFrancisco.com

Introduction

Society portrays a very vivid image that engulfs the intellect to perceive that the definition of one's success is based on what one's outer appearance looks like. Television advertisements, magazine advertisements, billboard signs, fashion runways, reality television shows, and the top model reality programs all paint portraits of success by merits based on the name brand of clothing that we wear, the expensive handbags that we carry (even if it is a knock-off), the cars we drive, or the gated communities that we live in.

Unfortunately, my sisters, these are measurements of success that many of us are guilty of utilizing. Don't act snooty; you are guilty, and I must admit, I am too. We provide free advertisement for every successful clothing and accessory line available. Our costly handbags, bling-bling jewelry, Jimmy Choo shoes, Mac make-up, St. John Knits, and even the line of lingerie we wear shouts, "Look at me; I have got it going on!" Honestly, we may look like we have it going on based on our outer appearance, but truth be told, there is a crisis going on inside of many women. We become so entangled in our appearance, or the appearances we portray before others, that we do not consider who we really are.

Regrettably, many women lose their focus in the midst of their journey because of overwhelming circumstances. As a result, their need for encouragement can manifest itself in various forms. For some women, a makeover may be encouraging while other women may only require an indulgent confection to do the trick. On the other hand, some women may find a stroll to the local mall is the thing needed to lift their spirits. A trip to my favorite upscale mall, a makeover, and a hot fudge brownie *a la mode* makes me feel a whole lot better about myself. Wait, add a massage to that list! Ironically, it was a trip to the mall that made me realize I was totally focusing on the outer Arlicia and not on my inner-self.

My teenage daughters, Lyndsey and Wendy, had requested a trip to the mall as they so often desired. Knowing that I was there to provide transportation and payment services for the various things on their list, I made my way into the local Victoria's Secret store to treat myself to a set of intimates. I am the kind of woman who just has to wear a matching set of intimates. I don't know about you, but I always feel better with a matching set on. No matter what is going on around me, it's just something about wearing that matching set that makes me feel better about myself. I have loved the television commercials and magazine advertisements which suggest that the merchandise Victoria's Secret sells is 'the best kept secret in town' for years. Wearing Victoria's Secret intimates and lingerie makes me feel better and look better; at least so I thought. According to their ads, you will feel sexier in their Very Sexy Collection, the bio-fit collection was custom made for you, their Perfect One Collection states smoothness like no other bra in the world, and the VS Collection has a silky, soft finish to it. Depending on your needs, Victoria's Secret has a collection that will keep your flaws hidden and your shortcomings a SECRET.

Unfortunately, Victoria's Secret does not offer anything to deal with the bumps and bruises of life. Let's just be honest, life happens. Victoria's Secret has a lot of merchandise to offer, but it does not offer solutions for the good, the bad, and the ugly of life that happen to the believer and the non-believer. We have no problem handling the good that life offers;

it's the bad and the ugly that present issues for us. What is the secret to handling the situations that we face day after day? You know, the situations that a makeover just can't cover up. How do you handle it when your husband announces he wants out after investing eighteen years in your marriage? What's the secret to coping with that? After a routine breast exam, the doctor discovers a lump that proves to be malignant. What is the secret to coping with that? A late bill turns into a disconnect notice, peanut butter and jelly sandwiches served on day-old-bread becomes your main entrée, and now your teenage son is walking with a twist and blinking his eyes every time he stresses a syllable. What is the secret to handling the madness that finds our address?

Okay, let's be honest. Women have so much to contend with every day. Women deal with marital issues, single issues, financial issues, educational issues, weight issues, social issues—the list of issues seems endless. I found myself looking for answers to my personal issues. Truth is, it was my own issues that led me to the merchandise in Victoria's Secret. Sickness in my body, my husband and I drifting apart, my teenage daughter trying to find herself, struggling to find balance for the many hats I wear daily, fading self-esteem, fake friends, and a family expecting me to hold everything together were just a few of my issues. I purchased lingerie that day thinking it would make me feel better. I thought a gift to myself would make my issues disappear. It wasn't until I had made my purchase that I discovered that my purchase was only a temporary resolve to my present situation. It was only after walking away with my pink bag in hand that the Lord spoke to me and said, "Victoria, isn't the only sister with a secret!"

While driving home, the Lord convicted me and showed me the need to be real with myself. I had issues and no matter how many matching bra and panty sets I bought, I was still searching for a solution. I began to search the Word of God for my solution, determined to seek the Lord for an answer. FINALLY *(isn't it funny how we go to God after we have tried everything else)*! It was then that I prayed for myself and began reading Scriptures to encourage myself. I ran into one of God's promises nestled away in the Old Testament book of Jeremiah: *"For I know the plans I have for you declares the Lord. plans to prosper you not to harm you, plans to give you hope and a future"* (Jeremiah 29:11, KJV). It was after reading and studying this text that I found the secret to handling the situations in my life. It was then I realized three things: (1) I have the secret, (2) I know the secret, and (3) I expect the secret to be revealed.

I am writing this book because so many women

suffering and hurting on the inside are looking for temporary help. If we are all honest, at some point, or another, there is a Victoria inside each of us reading this publication. Rich or poor, fat or skinny, Ph.D. or GED, married or single, the Word of God has a solution to every issue we face. Let me introduce you to a young lady whom I met named Victoria.

Chapter 1
"Her Name Is Victoria"

Like most women, 23-year-old college student, Victoria, had big dreams and goals. She finally reached her senior year in college and began to see herself as an adult. Victoria maintained a minimum wage paying job at a local daycare center and lived at home with her parents while matriculating at the local university. By no means was she excited to still be home living with her mama and daddy, but it cost a fortune to stay on campus. These weren't the coolest living arrangements; but as long as she remained enrolled in school and worked to achieve her goals, her parents did not charge her rent. They paid her car note, paid her car insurance, paid for maintenance on her car, and helped to purchase books after all of her grant money was gone. As much as Victoria hated living in her parents' home at the age of twenty-three, their financial provisions were the answers to her prayers. Day in and day out she made every effort to make the best of the situation. However, like most young people her age, she was so frustrated with having her parents constantly asking questions about her private life, snooping through the things in her bedroom, complaining if she came in after 2:00 A.M., and constantly nagging to remind her that she could never make it without their help.

Everywhere Victoria turned there was a reminder staring her in the face that she could not make it on her own. Not only did Victoria's parents render their opinions to her but to everyone else they knew. Her mother bragged to everyone she conversed with on the phone including her hairstylist, the pastor, the mail carrier, and Abdul (the Arabian gentleman who owned the corner store) that Victoria could not make it without their help. Granted, her parents were proud that they were in a position to help her. However, they completely took for granted that their nagging made her feel more like a burden than a blessing. Their remarks destroyed her self-esteem and made Victoria very resentful toward them.

Victoria graduated from high school five years ago, and the majority of her friends were all out on their own already. All she heard from her friends were the stories of the wild parties, card parties, and barbecues they were hosting every weekend. Her friend, Susan, even bragged about how wonderful it was not to have to answer to anyone except her live-in boyfriend. Her friend, Lori, bragged about how great it was not to have anyone ask her what time she would be home although she shared an apartment with three other ladies. And her friend, Jennifer, bragged about how she loved being able to invite her male friends over without having someone give them the third degree when they arrived. Thank God Jennifer had her own place because she had a different guy come over weekly. Usually, the male friend of the week stayed over until she got tired of him, and she found another weekend lover.

Victoria couldn't wait to have friends over to visit her very own place. She often strolled through the local superstore making decorating plans. As much fun as it was to spend hours daydreaming of how she would decorate her new place, the realization of actual costs was an instant dream killer! Victoria could daydream about having her own place all day long, but the reality of monthly rent, utilities, groceries, and money to keep gas in her car put her in a position to keep her mouth closed and put up with her parents' rules. As difficult as it was to face the truth, Victoria swallowed hard and returned to her parents' home day in and day out and listened to them remind her of how grateful she should be that they supported her.

The fall semester was finally behind her. With only one more semester to go, Victoria would be a college graduate. After a long day of taking three-year-olds to the potty, singing "Itsy Bitsy Spider," and having sand thrown in her hair, Victoria was tired and certainly not in the mood to deal with anymore drama. Victoria decided she would go home, shower, pour herself a cup of coffee, and watch a good movie. She arrived home, greeted her parents, and immediately entered her bedroom to prepare for a relaxing evening. She noticed that her mother had placed her mail on her dresser, and she began sorting through the magazines and bills to discover that her semester grades had arrived.

She was not worried about whether or not she passed, but she was praying the grade on her history term paper would boost her C average to at least a B average. With a loud "YES!" Victoria screamed after she had discovered she did earn a B average in her history course. With utter amazement, her father rushed into her room to ensure that everything was okay. Victoria calmed him down and shared with him her great news. Her father told her he was happy to see that she finally passed her history class and congratulated her on earning a B in her Algebra course. You see, this particular history class was a required course for Elementary Education majors and Victoria had failed it the first time and dropped it a second time. This was her third time taking the course, but this time she refused to be beaten by her past failures. Victoria answered her father with a smile and closed her room door.

As she proceeded to continue her relaxation plans, she wondered how it was that her father already knew she had passed the history course and had earned a B in her algebra course, seeing that she had not said a word to him previously. Victoria returned to her mail and discovered that the envelope had been previously opened. Her cell phone bill, department store bill, and credit card statements were opened as well. In total disbelief, Victoria asked her parents why they opened her mail. Her mother stated that she was worried about her grades, and if she failed she wanted to break the news to her gently. Her mother also said she wanted to know just how much money Victoria had spent on the new dress she wore to church on Sunday, because she was certain she paid entirely too much for it. After about twenty minutes of arguing, Victoria's father reminded her that this was his house and everything under his roof belonged to him and if she did not like it or the way he ran his house she could leave whenever she got good and ready. Her father reminded her AGAIN that they paid the car note, the insurance, kept the oil changed in the car, just bought new tires; and the books that helped her get that "B," they had paid for those, too. On top of that, she lived there for FREE!

With tears in her eyes, Victoria told her parents, "I am grateful for all you do, but it's wrong for you to open my mail and continue to go through my things. But, Dad, you are right. This is your house, and maybe it is time I leave." This argument was nothing new. As a matter of fact, they had this same argument at least once every other month. However, this was the first time Victoria announced that she had taken all she could take and would be leaving. Of course, her parents did not believe her, and honestly, Victoria couldn't believe she announced she was leaving; but she knew deep down in her heart it was time for her to go. It wasn't until she began boxing up her things that her parents realized she was really going to leave this time. Of course, they apologized and begged her to stay, but the time had come for her to move on with her life. Victoria was excited about the decision she made. For her, the decision didn't mean moving on, it meant moving on up!

Chapter 2

Moving On Up!

Victoria felt good about herself. She had achieved a major accomplishment. She was proud to whip out her key and unlock the door to her very own place. When she walked into her apartment on the third level of her building, Victoria sang the lyrics to the classic sitcom, *the Jeffersons*: *Well, we're moving on up, to the East side, to a deluxe apartment in the sky. Moving on up, to the East side, we finally got a piece of the pie.* And that's just how she felt. She felt as though she had a piece of the struggling college student's dream: a place of her own. With the beauty of earth tone paintings and ceramic designs, Victoria's "Diva Pad" was a mirror image of her personality. Every room in her new apartment was a reflection of her. It had only been three months since the blowout between Victoria and her parents. Even though she was struggling, Victoria was confident that moving out and moving up was the best decision she could have ever made.

Things were tough and within three months, she soon discovered that money leaves your hand a lot faster than it gets in your hands. Since it was Christmas break, Victoria took another job working as a cashier at the local grocery store. She planned to work all the hours she could, to save as much as she could to keep the bills paid during her last school semester. She worked 8 A.M. – 6 P.M., Monday through Friday, at the daycare center, and worked 7 P.M. – 12 A.M., Wednesday through Sunday, at the grocery store. This schedule left her working seven days a week. This crazy work schedule did not leave Victoria with one free day to enjoy her new fully furnished and HGTV-inspired decorated apartment. She had hoped that the second job would give her a nice little nest egg to hold on to, but she did not plan on having to buy a new car battery. Neither did she know that the light company required a $250.00 deposit and the apartment complex required her to pay the first and last month's rent up front. Advanced payments? Victoria had never heard of such a thing.

The more she thought she was ahead, the more she discovered she was just that much further behind. She found herself still scanning groceries in March. Was it really March already? Yes, it was March 1st, the rent was due, and the light bill too! Not only was she having money problems, but her grades were suffering as well. It was the spring semester, and she still had not graduated. Somehow her goals and dreams had taken a back seat. She no longer had the drive she once had to finish her goals. Her self-esteem was wounded. Victoria found herself taking a pill to go to sleep at night and a pill to remain awake during the day. Yes, she had her own place, but now she worried all the time. She worried about how she would pay this bill and that bill. The bills kept coming and Victoria was not mentally, physically, or financially prepared for the burden that came along as a result of her lease agreement.

It wasn't long before Victoria found herself leaving the minor care unit with a diagnosis she could not pronounce, headed to the pharmacy with a prescription she could not afford, and doctor's orders to take three days off from work. Simply put, the doctor's diagnosis meant Victoria needed to take a break before she began to break! As much as she hated to be off from work, Victoria had to admit her body really needed to rest. However, the time to rest just gave Victoria time to worry. She was worried about her bills and prayed to God that He would send a miracle angel to help her with her failing grades. After visiting her academic advisor, Victoria decided to withdraw from school and complete her requirements over the summer semester. Instead of graduating this spring semester, she would graduate a few months later in the summer. Not quite the academic plan she had in place, but she was determined not to allow this minor set-back to keep her from achieving her goals. Breaking the news to her parents was another story.

As expected, they were saddened. However, after realizing the summer semester began in only a few months, her parents were able to adjust to her new deadline. The adjustment also rendered a long speech of what she should have done differently. You guessed it; they argued AGAIN! Victoria was sick of hearing them constantly bash her. No matter what she did, they were never pleased. When would things ever change with them? No matter what she did, they griped and complained. Even after a trip to the minor care unit and with a prescription in her hand, her parents still fussed and fought. This time the argument led her to pack up her things, transfer her college credits, and with only a few dollars in her hands, leave the state of Texas and make the peach state of Georgia her new home. Victoria had planned to move to Atlanta after graduation but decided this was a wonderful opportunity to regroup and move as far away from her parents as she could. She did not know a soul in Atlanta but was not afraid of meeting new people. She made contacts and landed a job on campus at the childcare center. The salary they offered her was more than what she made working the previous jobs at the daycare and the grocery store back home. Things were looking up for Victoria. She was able to rent an apartment only two blocks from her new university, which meant she could walk to both school and work to save even more money.

It wasn't until she moved in that she soon discovered the cost of living in the city, the state capital of Georgia no less, was extremely expensive. Everything cost more. The salary that she thought was so great, suddenly wasn't enough to maintain her basic expenses. Victoria could not believe that she would need to find a second job again to make ends meet. The semester had not begun, so where would she get the money to buy the books her grant money didn't cover? On top of that, the out-of-state fees were horrendous. How dare the state penalize you for not being a resident to be able to attend their university? She could not believe that she was back in the same predicament she tried to run away from. This was not how things were supposed to go for her. As much as she hated it, Victoria knew a second job and working seven days a week was the solution to her problem. Once again, she found herself wearing an ugly green smock and scanning groceries, one canned good after another, to that annoying beeping sound. This was certainly not the "I can't wait until I am grown and on my own life" that she desired so much in high school. However, as hard as things were, Victoria had her mind made up to make the best of it because she would never move back home to Texas and face her parents' 'I told you so' faces again. Things were tough, but she embraced the "when the going gets tough, the tough get going" attitude and decided to just make the best of the situation.

Chapter 3
Decisions, Decisions, Decisions

Decisions, decisions, decisions! Being on your own also meant you were responsible for making one decision after the other. Making decisions really isn't that bad. The worst part of the decision is learning to live with the consequences of your choices whether good or bad. Unfortunately, Victoria was not making the best decisions right now. The fall semester had come and gone, and she was not enrolled in school. She had lost her grant money and would have to reapply for assistance in the spring semester. Victoria was still working two jobs and making only enough money to live paycheck to paycheck. She found herself taking more pills to get a good night's sleep and more pills to remain awake throughout the course of a day.

The decision to return to school later was one of the worst decisions she could have ever made. The financial rut she found herself in would not get any better without a better paying job. Her chances of finding a better paying job were slim to none without having a bachelor's degree in her hand. It was no secret that the more education you have, the more money you can expect to be paid. With a pen in hand, Victoria sat in the break room of the grocery store trying to write out another plan of action to move her closer to the goals she set for herself. Frustrated and disgusted, Victoria returned to register 7 wearing that ugly green smock and scanning groceries, one canned good after another, to that annoying beeping sound. She hated the first of the month! Ugh! Who needs this many canned goods?

Victoria's shift would end in ten more minutes. After scanning Mrs. Tate's frozen food items, it would be time to go home, or so Victoria thought. There was one more customer in her line before she could close her lane. Thank God he only had six items. Just as she scanned the last item, the customer threw a business card on her conveyor belt. Victoria looked up and asked the customer if he found everything O.K. Much to her surprise the customer was wearing a lime green suit, with a lime green trench coat, a lime green hat and a pair of lime green gators with a pipe hanging out of his mouth. It took everything for

Victoria not to laugh at the man dressed like a leprechaun. This man resembled the character, Lenny, off the latest episode of the sitcom *Good Times*.

Victoria wondered how in the world he jumped out of the television screen and into her line. The Mr. Lenny look-alike pulled out a wad of money and asked Victoria if she was sick of her dead-beat job. He asked if she was tired of long hours for little pay and no benefits. He wondered if she was tired of struggling to make ends meet and promised her a job to provide her with a life of luxury. Victoria snickered and asked the Lenny look-alike what kind of job he was offering. You didn't have to be a rocket scientist to know he was talking about prostitution. Shaking her head and laughing she responded, "Naw, I'm good."

Victoria could not believe she was approached by a real pimp. She continued to laugh as she turned off her register light and cleaned her conveyor belt in preparation for tomorrow. She was about to spray the conveyor belt down with cleanser when she picked up the pimp's business card and said to herself, "I wonder…" With a blank stare on her face, she placed the card in the pocket of her ugly green smock and proceeded to the time-clock to call it a day.

Victoria returned home to a stack of bills, a red disconnect notice for her unpaid light bill, and her incomplete financial aid package that was due in the morning. She needed to keep working on her plan of action, so she took out her journal to continue writing. She reached in her green smock pocket searching for a pen when she pulled out the business card the pimp left on her conveyor belt. The card read "Mr. Jackson – CEO of Global Enterprises." *Global Enterprises? Just what kind of business is Global Enterprises?* She had never heard of Global Enterprises. Victoria wondered what skills were needed for the job that the pimp was offering and just how much money the pimp was paying. She wondered what kind of benefits a pimp could possibly offer her. Victoria thought for a minute and wondered what she had to lose by calling Mr. Jackson and inquiring about the position.

Victoria telephoned Mr. Jackson and in a matter of days, innocently inquiring Victoria became an employee of Global Enterprises. She worked fewer hours and made more money than she could have ever imagined in her life. The salary of a prostitute outweighed the money she would have ever made with a degree in hand by a long shot. This lifestyle afforded her a luxury car, penthouse apartment, designer handbags, and the money to shop and purchase whatever she desired. It wasn't until the very first time she tried to decline an appointment from Mr. Jackson that she soon discovered, yes, she now possessed all the money she could have ever wanted, but she had also become the property of Global Enterprises.

The two bruises on her face were constant reminders that she was never to refuse him, and she was to do as she was told. Her life was not her own. She belonged to Mr. Jackson. Victoria could not make plans for herself; Mr. Jackson did. He made sure he got his money's worth out of her. What appeared to be a life of luxury, fortune, and fame quickly became a life of total disgrace. Victoria's life answered the question she asked herself only months earlier: what did she have to lose? The decision to make this one phone call caused her to lose everything she had. Victoria lost her self-respect, her self-esteem, her self-worth, her dignity, her dreams, her hopes, her destiny, her identity, her values, and her ambition.

Chapter 4
I Need A Plan

How is it possible to have everything a girl could ever want, but yet have nothing at all? Victoria sat on the deck of her penthouse apartment gazing at the beautiful high rise view. The life she was living was every girl's dream; but the hidden secrets she had to deal with were really every girl's nightmare. Dressed in a beautiful designer sundress and sandals while curled up on her chaise lounge sipping peach tea, Victoria couldn't help but wonder where her life went wrong. Her dream early in life was to graduate from college, land a job teaching school, and make her parents proud of her. But for the last three years she had told them one lie after the other.

As Victoria sat there in disgust, she had to admit to herself that she did have a few things that made her proud. She drove a convertible luxury car, she lived in a luxury penthouse apartment in the heart of

Atlanta, several of her handbags cost more than her monthly lease, and she had a different pair of red bottom shoes for every day of the month. She was able to purchase things that most women only dreamed of having. While her possessions were enough to make her proud, the reality of how she achieved those things made her sick to her stomach.

Victoria had to admit to herself that she had become the woman everyone talked about and the woman every woman hates. How in the world did this happen to her? She had a strong desire to make her parents proud, but the reality of what she did for a living would literally kill her God-fearing parents. How in the world could she ever tell them that she sold her body to get ahead in life? How could she ever go to her class reunion and face her classmates, knowing that she had become the girl that gave it up? How could she sit in the hair salon and read about herself in the books and magazines on the shelf? Even worse, how could she admit to herself that she was another man's property? The truth began to eat away at Victoria. And as much as she loved having a host of wonderful things and the money to buy whatever she wanted, what she desired most was to have her life back.

An overloaded mind and the sound of the water trickling from the waterfall on her beautiful balcony caused Victoria to fall asleep while lounging in her chaise lounge. Two hours later, she was awakened to a phone call from her mother. Victoria's busy lifestyle and the guilt and shame she carried on the inside caused her to be very distant with family. But her mother did not let that come between them. Mother Stevens called Victoria every Wednesday evening to check on her, to encourage her to come home for a visit, and to *please* go to church. Tonight's phone call was no different. Startled by her mother's ringtone, Victoria knew this was her weekly check-in call to say how proud her parents were and to inquire with great hopes about her upcoming graduation from a school she was not even enrolled in; but tonight, Mother Stevens had a little more to say.

Tonight, Mother Stevens did not allow Victoria to rush her off the phone like she usually did. Tonight's phone call was quite different.

Mother Stevens said, "Victoria, you know our plans and God's plans are not the same. Baby, the plans we make in life never look like God's plans. Is this life you're living the plan God has for you, or is this the life Victoria planned that she is still trying to figure out?"

Victoria listened as her mother continued, "You

know I don't have a college degree, but I know the Word of God, baby! Victoria, go get your Bible and read Jeremiah 29:11. God has a plan for your life, and if you just ask Him, He will show you. Pray to God and He will reveal it to you, baby! Victoria, you know sometimes we get in God's way trying to do things on our own, and we mess up the blessings God had intended for our life. But when you mess up, all you have to do is pray and ask God to lead you and guide you, and He will put you back on track. I woke up this morning praying for you as I always do."

Mother Stevens shared with her daughter, "The Lord told me to call you and remind you that HE has a plan and all you have to do is trust HIM and He will work it out. Victoria, put your hand in God's hand. No other man is going to lead you and take care of you like God can. Just trust Him, baby. He will do it. Mama knows. I've been trusting Him for seventy-two years, and He has not failed me yet. Pray about it, and God will fix it. Mama loves you, and I will always be here for you. Now when are you coming home to visit? You haven't been home in nearly three years? And when is graduation? I bought a real nice white suit to wear to your graduation. Your Dad says he is going to wear that same black suit. He needs a new black suit. He wants to be buried in that old thing!"

Mother Stevens laughed and said, "Call me and let me know when graduation is so your Dad and I can come witness our baby walk across that stage."

Something about her mother's telephone call tonight was different. Victoria did not just hear her mother, but she really listened to what she had to say tonight. With her face drowned in tears, Victoria thanked her mother and said she would call her soon with her graduation date. As she hung up the phone, Victoria knew her mother may have made the phone call, but it was actually the Lord speaking to her through her mother. This luxurious call-girl lifestyle was not what the Lord had planned for her life. Finally, after three years of being used and abused by men she didn't know, Victoria finally knew she had to leave this lifestyle. Now how she would leave Global Enterprises was another subject. Her boss, or should I say, her pimp, Mr. Carl Jackson, had already warned her that she was his property. Victoria knew there was only one person who could help her, and that was the Lord. Victoria went inside and called in dinner from her favorite Chinese Restaurant.

Sitting at her dinner table all alone, eating Chinese take-out on fine china and sipping on a glass of fine wine, the words of Mother Stevens begin to echo in her lonely penthouse. Victoria could not remember everything her mother said verbatim, but she remembered that her mother encouraged her to trust God and no other man, and she remembered that her mother said God had a plan for her life. Victoria was puzzled trying to figure out the plan God had for her and how would she know what the plan was.

She knew that the life she was living was definitely not what God had planned for her. She knew enough about God to know that He definitely did not plan for any child of His to be a prostitute; that's for sure. Victoria spent hours sitting at the dinner table trying to figure out what was God's plan for her life, and wondering how could she get a copy of God's plan for her life. She was too proud to call her mother and ask her what to do. Victoria finally got up from the dinner table, washed the dishes, showered, and prepared herself for bed. She sat on the edge of her bed still trying to figure out how in the world do I get a copy of God's plan when she heard her mother's voice say, *"Victoria, go get your Bible and read Jeremiah 29:11. God has a plan for your life, and if you just ask Him, He will show you. Pray to God, and He will reveal it to you, baby."* Once again she heard her mother say, *"Victoria, go get your Bible and read Jeremiah 29:11. God has a plan for your life, and if just ask Him, He will show you. Pray to God, and He will reveal it to you baby."* The instructions: Go get your Bible, read, and pray became very clear to her.

Victoria went to the shelf and pulled out her Bible and her journal. She found Jeremiah 29:11 and read aloud, *"For I know the plans I have for you,"* declares the Lord. *"Plans to prosper you not to harm you, plans to give you hope and a future."* Reading the Scripture did not tell her exactly what the plans were; and that frustrated Victoria all the more. She wanted to know exactly what the Lord had planned for her life. Why isn't the Bible just a little more specific? Couldn't the Lord have just spelled it out? Victoria decided to follow her mother's instructions to the letter. I have read the Scripture; now I will pray and see what God has to say.

That night Victoria fell on her knees and prayed before she got in her bed. She prayed, "Lord I need You! My life is a mess and only You can fix it! Today, I start over by giving my life to You totally. Lord, I need You to have Your way in every area of my life. I am sorry for my sinful lifestyle and the way I have been living. Honestly, Lord, I knew better, but I thought my way was better than Yours and, Lord, I was wrong. I want out of this call-girl lifestyle, and I know Mr. Jackson will not let me go, but I know my life belongs to You. It was You who gave me my life; it was You, Lord, who brought me into this world, not Mr. Jackson! I am afraid of him, but I know he has no power to keep my life. So I am begging You, Lord, to forgive me and free me of this sinful lifestyle.

Lord, I want a fresh start. I want to start-over with You! Please make a way, Lord! Starting today, I want the plan You have for my life! I trust You and the plans You have for my life, to prosper me and not to harm or hurt me. You promised, Lord, and I am standing on Your promises! Forgive me, Lord! I love you!"

With a made up mind to trust God, Victoria climbed in bed and began writing the plans in her journal as she heard from the Lord. The Lord kept Victoria up for hours writing the plans He had destined for her life. The Lord had given her instructions to move out of the luxury penthouse, return to school to complete her educational goals, reunite with her family, and return to church. Victoria did not know how she would complete everything the Lord instructed her to do. However, she knew that it must be done and she had to start her life over again. This time, she was starting her life over with God on her side!

Chapter 5
Sometimes You Have to Start Over!

A decision to start over often appears as a sign of failure; but it all depends on how you look at the situation. Starting over can be the solution in the equation of success. To many, it may have appeared that Victoria's decision to start her life over was a major setback. Downsizing from her 1,680 square-foot penthouse in Atlanta, Georgia, to a one-bedroom apartment, all of 450 square feet back in her hometown in Texas was quite a change but the truth is, it was a good change. This apartment did require an access code to open the gate, but there wasn't the added luxury of an attendant there to greet you every day. This apartment did not have marble floors and granite counter tops, but it did have a ceramic floor entry way. There was no walk-in closet where all of her clothes were color coordinated, and her shoes were no longer stored in clear shoe boxes with a description label on the outside. This apartment did not have a walk-in shower with shower heads so massive they could clean cars in a car wash. As a matter of fact, Victoria's new apartment was short on a few amenities. No dishwasher, no washing machine, no dryer, no alarm system, no flat screen television in every room, and no waterfall on the balcony. She did have a balcony at this apartment, but it was only large enough for one chair and a little round barbecue grill she often cooked on to save on her light bill expenses.

Starting over for Victoria not only included a change in address, but a change in every aspect of her life. She traded in her Mercedes Benz for a Toyota. Instead of ordering take-out she cooked her meals, did her own laundry, became her own maid, and did her own manicures and pedicures. Victoria now went to work Monday through Friday and really enjoyed her job as a teacher's assistant. She was back working in her field of study and getting the experience she needed as a teacher. Although there was a major difference in the money she made, Victoria managed to keep her bills paid and saved a little money on the side. Life was certainly different for Victoria, and although she couldn't explain it, life was really good. There were moments when it appeared to her that she had less, but she actually had so much more.

Victoria couldn't explain it; but she knew a change had certainly come her way.

For the last six years of her life, Victoria and her parents had drifted apart. As a matter of fact, she had become so distant with her family that her kin folk had nearly forgotten what she looked like. She had not been to any of the family reunions; she did not show up for Uncle Joe's funeral (he was her only uncle on her father's side of the family); she did not even come home when her mother had knee replacement surgery. For the last six years, Victoria had nearly walked away from her family, friends, and life altogether. Her life had revolved around Mr. Carl Jackson and Global Enterprises; he had become her only sense of family.

Victoria's decision to start her life over helped her to repair and restore the relationship with her parents. She did not move back into her parents' home, but she did make a point to visit her parents weekly and call her mother at least two or three times a week. Victoria realized that her parents only wanted the very best for their only child. For the first time since her high school graduation, Victoria was involved in her church, and she loved every minute of it. Years had gone by since the last time that she felt like she could not wait to not go to church. She couldn't wait to stay home on a Sunday evening and watch Lifetime movies all day. She thought she was going to love driving to the park every Sunday afternoon to be with her friends. But now her life was different, and she knew she needed to be back in church.

After missing nearly six years of attending church, Victoria made her way to Salem Missionary Baptist Church and became a faithful member. Victoria got actively involved in the Greeters' Ministry and loved greeting the members and visitors every Sunday morning. Victoria stood at the West entrance of the church greeting everyone who came through that door with her Greeters' Ministry badge, a smile on her face, a warm handshake, and a hug. Victoria's involvement in the church pleased her parents. Her parents were extremely proud to have her back in the church and working to complete her goals. Victoria could not explain it, but her setback was a stage for a strong comeback in her life.

Starting over provided Victoria with a sense of peace, if nothing else. Yes, things were quite different in her life. There was a major difference in where she lived, what she drove, the friends she entertained, and even the clothes she wore. Victoria could no longer afford to shop the luxurious name brand stores, but you would never know it on Sunday mornings. She kept most of her expensive shoes, all of her name brand handbags, and she didn't dare part with her St. John's suits. She did sell a few things during her moving sale, but she refused to sell all of her good stuff. She may have been broke as shattered glass, but you could never tell by looking at her. Besides it would have cost her to replace all of her clothing. Not only did she continue to dress well, but inner peace had overtaken her. Victoria found spiritual and psychological peace within herself. The restored relationship with God, her family, and her church family had changed Victoria. She could now say, "This JOY that I have, the world didn't give it and the world can't take it away!" Well, so, she thought.

Chapter 6

You Can Run But You Can't Hide

A decision to start over and make a change also involves a decision to change your surroundings. Think about it: A person who decides to diet will never lose weight if he continues to dine at the buffet. Just the idea of being able to have it all is just too tempting.

Victoria applied change to every aspect of her life. She found new friends at church and now socialized only at church and family events. This was a major change from her previous party-girl lifestyle. Instead of night clubs and hotel parties after the Atlanta Falcons game, Victoria now found joy at her post serving on the Greeters' Ministry and helping in the Hospitality Ministry at church. She had a past that she wanted to forget and never be reminded of, but she was constantly questioned about her decision to move back to Texas. Anytime she ran into a classmate of hers the question was always raised: Why did you move back home? Victoria always used the excuse of being an only child as her reason for returning home. She would always remind others that her parents were aging, and she needed to be closer to home to take care of them. As true as her statement was, the real truth was Victoria was running from her past. She constantly prayed that no one would ever discover her previous lifestyle. She knew that her parents would be crushed and her reputation ruined if anyone ever found out she used to be a call-girl.

Mr. Jackson had promised that he would find her if she ever tried to leave him. As much as she tried not to think about it, she was always afraid he would reappear in her life. Victoria took precautions in securing her identity. She changed her cellular number and moved to a suburb near her hometown. The twenty minutes commute to visit her parents and attend church was a bit much but well worth the ability to keep her identity a secret. Victoria knew that her life would be over if Mr. Jackson was ever able to locate her.

It had nearly been a year since her move, and Victoria thought she was safe from the life of Global

Enterprises until one fateful Tuesday evening when she walked into her parents' home and found a beautiful bouquet of red roses on the kitchen table. Victoria began to tease her mother about her father still sending her flowers. Mother Stevens informed Victoria that the flowers were not from her dad, but were in fact, delivered here for her! In total amazement, Victoria asked her mother why in the world she would purchase flowers for her; it wasn't her birthday or anything. It was then her mother gave her the attached card and with a big grin on her face she said, "Just read it. You have a secret admirer!" Victoria felt her stomach turn when she opened the card and read: "You can run, but you can't hide! Coming for you. Carl."

Her mother said, "They are from that Carl Jackson guy, aren't they?"

Victoria stood there and looked as if she had been hit by a meteor falling from the sky! Her excited mother said, "Sweetie, I forgot to tell you one of your classmates, Carl Jackson, left a message for you to call him a couple of weeks ago."

Victoria immediately thought surely not THE Carl Jackson? Please, Lord, NO! Not THE Carl Jackson of Global Enterprises? Victoria knew there was no classmate named Carl Jackson. The leprechaun had found her! Oh, Lord, No!

Her mother continued, "He said he will be in town next week and wants to meet you for lunch or dinner. He said he had been trying to get in touch with you for nearly a year. He had no idea that you had moved back home from Atlanta. He called again this morning and asked for your address to send you flowers. I wouldn't give him your new address, but I told him to send them here that you would be by later on today."

Victoria asked her mom if she had given him her number to reach her and her mother said, "No, I didn't give him your cell number, but I did take down his number and I told him I would give you the message to call him. He said he would love to take you to lunch or dinner so you guys could catch up on old times. He was a real inquisitive young man and wanted to know so much about you. I thought that was so nice and told him you would call him soon to catch up. I don't remember him, but I am sure you do. Isn't that nice, Victoria? Let me see, where did I put his number?"

Victoria sat in dead silence. Hell, NO! This was not nice! As a matter of fact, it was the worst thing that could have ever happened to her. Victoria always feared that Mr. Jackson would come looking for her and deep down on the inside she knew he would use her mother to locate her. What if he harmed her parents? He was a monster, and Victoria knew it. It was as if she didn't hear a word her mother was saying. She feared this day would come and finally her worst fear had become a reality. What would she do now? He knew where her mother lived and for all she knew he could be parked outside her mother's house waiting to attack her. What in the world was she going to do now?

Victoria spent the remainder of the evening in a daze. It was as if her life had become that Sunday afternoon Lifetime movie. It took her nearly two hours to drive her normal twenty minutes drive home. For all she knew, Mr. Jackson or some of his goons were watching every move she made. She kept looking over her shoulders. She was annoyed and irritated every time she looked in her rear view mirror and saw the bouquet of flowers strapped in the back seat belt of her car. Her mother wanted to make sure the roses arrived home safely, so she buckled them in the seat belt. The flowers had to go. For all she knew a tracking device could have been attached to them.

It wasn't until the low fuel light in her car began blinking that she realized she was almost out of gas. This brought Victoria's runaway drive to a halt and provided the perfect opportunity to get the flowers out of her car. The last thing she needed in her apartment was a reminder of Carl Jackson. Victoria walked into the Valero gas station and told the clerk, "Today is your day," and left the bouquet of flowers on the counter for the young lady. The store clerk said, "Thank you! I love roses!" The young lady asked why in the world she would give away a bouquet of beautiful red roses. The clerk said, "He has either cheated on you, married, or gay, which is it?" Victoria looked at her and said, "It's my secret, and I'll never tell. Enjoy the flowers."

There isn't a woman alive who wouldn't appreciate a bouquet of red roses from her man; but when the man is a pimp chasing you down, no woman would dare keep those flowers. Victoria thought about calling the police and asking for protection but what would she say, "Help! My pimp is after me" and let the police know she was a former prostitute? She couldn't tell her father, and she could not tell any of her friends from church. If she would dare tell anyone that she needed protection, she would have to answer the 'who, what, when, where, and why' questions. There was no way Victoria was about to utter one word of this secret. For years, she heard her mother make wise cracks that others better hope the Lord was taking a nap while they were doing their dirt, and He missed what they were doing. This was one time Victoria hoped her mother's wise crack was true. She could only hope that she had hidden her dirt from the Lord, but she knew this was one secret she had kept from everyone but God. Only the Lord knew of her secret lifestyle.

After making it safely into her apartment, Victoria locked her apartment door and jammed a chair under the doorknob. She prepared herself for bed and continued her nightly routine of reading her Bible and writing in her journal. It was nearly a year ago that she really took the advice of her mother and began to seek God for the plans for her life. There were many days when Victoria found herself frustrated because she still did not know exactly what God had planned for her life, and after tonight she was almost certain there was a default in God's plan. Why would God allow this to happen to her? The Scripture clearly reads that God had plans to prosper you and not to harm you, plans to give you hope and a future. Either the Lord was just downright picking on her or there was a default in His Word. If the Lord had all these wonderful plans then how did she end up being a call-girl running from a man dressed in a lime green suit looking like a leprechaun on St. Patrick's Day? True, the money she made was great, but there certainly wasn't anything prosperous about that lifestyle. And where was this future that God said He had for her? Was He really serious? She could not see anything great in her future. There was nothing great about being locked inside an apartment with a chair jammed under the doorknob? What kind of future was this?

This lifestyle definitely wasn't a future worth bragging on. Victoria wanted to give up on God. She began to feel as though she had wasted an entire year of her life. All year long she had been asking God what His plan was for her life, and she still did not know. Victoria thought the Lord would have an answer within 365 days. She followed her mother's instructions carefully: *"Victoria, go get your Bible and read Jeremiah 29:11. God has a plan for your life, and if you just ask Him, He will show you. Pray to God, and He will reveal it to you, baby."* The instructions: Go get your Bible, read, and pray had become a part of Victoria's new lifestyle. Every night she read her Bible, wrote in her journal, and prayed to God, seeking His plan for her life and now the lack of results had her frustrated with God and her mother. Victoria began to think that God and her mother were working together to see her make a fool out of herself while she was waiting to hear His plans.

Chapter 7
I Need Thee

Victoria spent the entire day looking over her shoulders. All day long she wondered if someone was watching her and waiting to snatch her at a moment's notice. Victoria knew Mr. Jackson's history with other girls who tried to leave his Global Enterprise Business. She remembered how he hunted Sabrina down and had his goons drag her back. As a reminder never to leave him again, Sabrina's car was set afire. She had vivid memories of the bruises Amber had all over her arms and the black eye she received when she was found two years after trying to run away. Victoria knew the kind of monster he was and was certain he would harm her and anything or anyone close to her to remind her that she would be his property for the rest of her life.

Unlike Sabrina and Amber, Victoria was also Mr. Jackson's lover. Suga, as he affectionately called her, and she was his prized possession. Her beauty and shapely body were the assets every man dreamed of, and Mr. Jackson knew this first hand. Mr. Jackson took good care of Victoria financially. While all of the other girls received 25% of what they brought in, Victoria was the only girl who received 35%, and the penthouse apartment she once lived in was an added bonus. Mr. Jackson bought Victoria every name brand shoe, handbag, and line of clothing you could think of and had a wardrobe for every season and every occasion. He always bought her the best of everything, and because she had the wealthiest clients, he made a load of money off of Victoria.

Some of the wealthiest men in Atlanta requested to spend their time and money on Victoria. Victoria was the secret lover of many of the professional football players, doctors, high profile lawyers, pastors, and businessmen. The other girls brought in business, but nothing like Victoria. When she moved away, several of his best clients took their business to the streets. Mr. Jackson tried to convince them his other girls were pleasers, but none of them could replace the beauty and poise of Victoria.

Thoughts of what he would possibly do to her frightened her and had her scared for her life. She had spent the entire day at work scared. After a long day of dealing with whining children, she walked to her car in fear and raced home. Victoria drove again constantly looking back in the rear view mirror to see if she was being followed. Victoria felt like she was a criminal on the run from the police. This was crazy! She gave a sigh of relief as she returned to her apartment safely.

Victoria wanted to attend mid-week worship like she did every Wednesday night, but this Wednesday she was really afraid to even walk out of her apartment door. She sat on the couch jumping at every sound she heard. She kept walking back and forth looking out of the window and checking to make sure the chair was jammed under the door knob. She began to wonder just how long she would have to live in fear of this man. What kind of life was this for her to live? It was 6:15 P.M. Mid-week service started at 7:00 P.M., and if she was going to make it, she would have to make a decision and leave now. Victoria felt that the church was one of the safest places she could go. She gave it no more thought. She grabbed her purse and made a dash to her car. Before she realized it, Victoria was at church with her hands lifted high in praise.

Although she was scared, going to church proved to be the best decision ever. The praise and worship team ushered the congregation to a high place, and Victoria totally forgot all about Mr. Jackson and her hidden secrets. The team sang the hymn "I Need Thee" and the church lost it! The power of the Holy Ghost was thick in the house that night. The congregation went into a place of praise and worship that was so high that the preacher did not have to preach. Rev. Albert followed the lead of the Holy Spirit and invited everyone who was seeking to hear from God to come to the altar for prayer. He encouraged those who needed the Lord to make a way, to make their way to the altar and tell God exactly what they needed. He instructed those who came for prayer to begin tonight's prayer by asking God to forgive them before making any request. Rev. Albert then encouraged the congregation to trust God. He said, *"Trust in the LORD with all thine heart; and lean not unto thine own understanding. In all thy ways acknowledge him, and he shall direct thy paths."*

Victoria needed to hear this message so badly. It was as if the Lord had a megaphone in His hand speaking directly for her to hear Him. Her mother had encouraged her to read her Bible and pray, and God would reveal His plan to her. Tonight the preacher encouraged the congregation to trust God, lean on Him, acknowledge Him and He will direct your path. She said that God has a plan for our lives, and we have to stay on course no matter what the road ahead may look like. Victoria prayed like she had never prayed before. She did not care who was looking at her or what others thought about her. She needed to hear from God, and she was tired of living in fear. Her prayer led into a repetitious cry of "I trust You! Lord, I trust You!" Over and again Victoria repeated these words and the more she prayed it aloud, the better she felt.

For over a year, Victoria had been seeking God's plans for her life and she honestly began to feel that her life was a total failure. The pain of her past had begun to eat away at her and now, after being discovered by her pimp, she was certain her secrets would hinder the plan that God had designed for her life. It was hard to admit, but Victoria knew deep down inside that she was paying for the bad choices she had made in her life. Rev. Albert spoke and offered the congregation words of encouragement. "We often make choices that will delay God's plan, but the redemptive road He provides will lead us to the road of victory which will not be denied." It was as if Victoria had received a breath of fresh air. Yes, she had made some bad decisions in her life, but tonight, she asked God to forgive her and she knew the Lord heard her.

Victoria walked away from the altar a renewed woman. She was ready to face her fears and was no longer ashamed of her past mistakes. She was sure there were others at church who had secrets of their own. Even Rev. Albert said if we were honest many of us have so many buried secrets in our closets that our closets look like graveyards. Victoria had no plans to dig her own dirt up but knew that the old saying was true: what's done in the dark will certainly come to light and no matter what, you can fool some people some of the time, but you can never fool God any of the time. It is what it is, and she would one day have to face reality, but Victoria refused to let Mr. Carl Jackson or anyone else steal her renewed spirit. Sunday was Family & Friends Day at her church, and Victoria had plans to enjoy her visiting family and her church family. She still feared having to come face to face with the secrets of her past, but she made up her mind that she would just have to deal with it head on.

Chapter 8
Don't I Know You?

Family & Friends Day was the buzz of the community. For months, all Victoria heard was how many people would be at the Family & Friends Day service. It seemed that everywhere she turned people were talking about Family & Friends Day at Salem Missionary Baptist Church. Victoria even overheard two ladies at the local superstore talking about how they were planning to get to church early to make sure they got a seat and a good parking space. In the beauty shop, some women were talking about the songs they had rehearsed at choir rehearsal and how the choir would be jamming.

For the Family & Friends Day service, their pastor invited his brother from Atlanta to be the guest preacher. Victoria had never heard her pastor's brother preach, but he must have been a great preacher because all she heard her mother talk about was how well Pastor's brother could preach. Victoria hadn't been to a Family & Friends Day service in years, but she was so excited about church that she gave no more thought to Mr. Carl Jackson. Victoria refused to allow the drama of her past to hinder the joy of rekindling her family relationships. She got so wrapped up into her family that she totally forgot that she was scared of him finding her. Victoria put all of her energy into making sure that everything went as her mother planned. She had not seen her mother this happy in a very long time. As a fund raiser, the church named the family with the most invited guests as "Family of the Year." Mother Stevens was sure that her family would win this year, so this was an especially big day for her family.

Mother Stevens was overjoyed that Victoria had moved back home and would be a part of this big day. Mother Stevens invited family members and friends they had not seen in years. This special occasion gave Mother Stevens a reason to host a family reunion and she was certain the Stevens family would walk away with the trophy and the prize cake. The Stevens family included family members whom Victoria did not even remember. Some of her relatives had taken vacation time and flew in from as far as California to attend the service and the big family reunion Mother Stevens had planned. Mother Stevens worked hard and planned a huge dinner for her 300 invited guests at the IBEW Hall, including the pastor and his visiting family from Atlanta, GA. Several of the men in the family had come over early Saturday and spent the whole day barbecuing. While the men were barbecuing several of the women worked to decorate the hall. The tables were decorated with black tablecloths and turquoise balloon centerpieces.

To make sure the event was well planned, Mother Stevens placed Victoria in charge of entertainment for the family reunion. While Mother Stevens hired a DJ and a moonwalk for the younger children to have entertainment, she had Victoria purchase numerous decks of cards, dominoes, checkers, and several other board games to help keep the family entertained for hours. Victoria also planned to have a scavenger hunt, dance contest, bingo, a cake walk, and drawings for door prizes. She was excited at the opportunity to reunite with her family. This was one busy Saturday in the Stevens household. Family members were checking into the hotel and running to the mall for last minute wardrobe purchases. People were going back and forth to the hall to help with final reunion plans and dropping off pies and cakes left and right. Victoria was beginning to think her mother invited the entire community to the family reunion dinner. It had been a long day, but the joy on her mother's face was worth it all. And to make her just that much happier, Victoria spent the night in her old room to be near her mother just in case she needed any last minute help.

It had been years since Victoria slept in her old bed. Victoria laid there with so many memories racing through her mind. She could hardly sleep thinking of the good times growing up in the Stevens' household. Victoria got up and walked around her old bedroom looking at all the pictures on the wall. Her mother had not changed one thing in her bedroom. The room was just like she left it before she moved to Atlanta. It was as if her mother had a shrine in her honor. Victoria believed her mother would have been the happiest if she would have lived with them for the rest of her life! Victoria began to go through her old things and found some of her clothing in her dresser drawers. She could not believe her mother had kept all of these things. Victoria opened her closet, and some of her clothing were still hanging in the closet. The dress she wore to the prom, her homecoming outfit, and several other outfits she had worn were still hanging in her closet. Even her old Letterman jacket was still in the closet. Victoria tried it on. She was amazed when she looked at herself in the mirror with her old Letterman's jacket on. Victoria kept the jacket on as she continued to take a stroll down memory lane right in the middle of her bedroom.

The pictures on the wall and in her yearbook forced Victoria to recall the plans she had for herself. Victoria went through the stack of yearbooks and photo albums of her years growing up. She picked up what she thought was another photo album and discovered it was a journal that her mother kept. After reading a few pages of the entries, Victoria figured out that her mother would come into her old bedroom every night to pray for her during her prayer time. In her journal she begged God to protect Victoria.

Victoria sat on the bed with tears in her eyes after reading the prayers that her mother had written. Her mother dated every entry and either wrote a prayer for her or logged her every attempt to communicate with her. She noticed that every time her mother called her, she logged it in the prayer journal. Most of the entries read: "Lord, please take care of my Vickie; she didn't answer the phone today, and she didn't call me back. I haven't talked to her, but let her know I love her. Lord, I know You will take care of my baby."

Tears continued to stream down Victoria's face as she read the prayers that her mother had written while she was out on the streets selling her body. She was embarrassed to read the countless entries where her mother had written "I didn't talk to her again today." It was one o'clock in the morning and Victoria was still seated on the edge of her bed dressed in her pajamas and her Letterman jacket reading her mother's prayer journal when Mother Stevens gracefully walked in and sat next to Victoria.

Mother Stevens placed her arm around Victoria and said, "One thing I know, God does answer prayers." Mother Stevens told Victoria how she never gave up on her and how she continued to pray and ask God to take care of her baby. She told her she knew that she would one-day return home. Mother Stevens said, "I know God has great plans for your life and one day you will discover that God's plans are not our plans. And God never fails!" It broke Victoria's heart to read how her mother worried about where she was and what she was doing. Victoria began to apologize for the grief she had caused her parents. She was just about to confess her call-girl lifestyle to her mother when Mother Stevens told her, "Vickie we all have secrets and some secrets are left between you and God. You don't have to tell me, just talk to God about it and ask Him to forgive you." Mother Stevens gave Victoria a big hug and told her, "It's way past our bedtime. We have a big day tomorrow and we both need some rest."

Finally, it was Sunday morning! Victoria got to church early and much to her surprise, everyone was right. People were coming from everywhere. She was glad there was a section reserved for the Greeters' Ministry, otherwise there wouldn't have been seats on the floor for them. They would have had to search the balcony or sit in the overflow room. Hug after hug, handshake after handshake, the church begin to fill to capacity. Victoria held a smile but was overcome by embarrassment every time her mother dragged a family member to her post to see her. Why couldn't this wait until after church? She could meet everybody at the hall they rented for the reunion lunch. Victoria was relieved when her mother told her she was going to her seat before she lost it. Within minutes, the Greeters' Ministry was also making their way to their seats when someone tapped Victoria on the shoulders.

Victoria turned around and to her amazement before her stood Attorney Nigel Albert from Atlanta, GA. Victoria thought she had seen a ghost.

Attorney Albert said, "WOW! Where have you been? I thought you had fallen off the face of the earth?"

Victoria had another I- have-just-been-hit-by-a-meteor-falling-from-the-sky moment. "What are you doing at my *church*?" she asked Nigel.

"My cousin is one of the ministers here and she

invited us." Attorney Albert gave Victoria a hug and whispered in her ear, "I still love you."

Victoria pushed away from him and turned around but ran into her mother. Nigel introduced himself to Mother Stevens as an old friend from Atlanta. Mother Stevens was so happy to meet a friend of Victoria's. She immediately invited Nigel to join their family for dinner after church. Victoria could not believe this but had no time to dwell on it. People were everywhere and began rushing to get seats. Before long, Mother Stevens was rushing Nigel along like a mother leading a two-year-old child in a large crowd.

Nigel was beginning to move through the maze-like crowd when he turned around and said, "Hey, have you seen Carl yet? He is going to be shocked to know you are here, too?"

Here, too? What did he mean 'here, too'? How did he know Mr. Carl Jackson had been in town? Victoria wondered if Attorney Albert knew that Mr. Jackson was looking for her. Victoria could not believe this. Nigel was one of Global Enterprises best clients. She had been his call-girl for several years. Victoria walked away thinking who would have ever imagined she would run into one of her clients at church.

Church was packed! And everyone had to agree, the choir was jamming! Victoria had just gotten the shock of her life, but church was too good for her to think about that. Not only was the choir jamming, but the praise dancers were dancing. Ladies were waving colorful flags from the front of the church all the way into the balcony. People were up clapping and singing along with the praise team. Victoria was amazed. She felt as though she was watching service on television. This wasn't the Family & Friends Day service she was accustomed to. Now she could see why everyone was getting hyped up about that special day. She was so glad to be a part of such a wonderful service she totally forgot about running into Nigel.

Victoria was up on her feet clapping her hands and having a wonderful time. She couldn't help but notice the joy on her mother's face during church service. She knew her presence today had made her mother the happiest woman on earth as her prayers had been answered: Victoria had returned to the church. Mother Stevens was so happy to have Victoria and all of her family in church together. Victoria couldn't help but cry when she saw the big smile on her mother's face. The lady, Vanessa, seated next to her dug in her purse and found a balled up tissue to wipe the tears and smeared mascara off Victoria's face. The running mascara on her face made Victoria look like a crying clown.

Vanessa wiped and wiped Victoria's face and finally suggested she hurry and run to the ladies' room to wash her face with some cold water to remove the running mascara before the guest preacher came into service. "You can make it back before the armor bearer has the guest preacher on the platform; you wouldn't miss anything."

Victoria took Vanessa's advice. She leaned over and asked Vanessa to please make sure no one sat in her seat, and she made a mad dash for the ladies' room. Victoria looked at herself in the mirror and thought she was staring at a character in a horror film. Her mascara had run down her entire face. And to think she paid $23 for a tube of no-run mascara.

Feeling refreshed and no longer looking like a horror movie character, Victoria rushed back to her seat. As she took her seat, the armor bearer was escorting the guest preacher on to the platform. The choir had just began singing their last selection to prepare the worshipers for the message to follow. Victoria thanked Vanessa for making sure her seat was saved. Vanessa looked her over and said, "Thank God for soap and water because you looked a hot mess!" The ladies laughed and got right back into worship, but Victoria's praise came to an immediate halt when she looked up on the platform. She had yet another, I-have-just-been-hit-by-a-meteor-falling-from-the-sky moment when she saw that the pastor's brother from Atlanta, GA., who was also the guest preacher for Family and Friends Day, was none other than Mr. Leprechaun himself, her former pimp, THE MR. CARL JACKSON.

Chapter 9
Colliding With Her Past

Not just, NO, but Hell, No! Victoria could not believe this! What in God's name was Carl Jackson doing in anybody's pulpit? Victoria stood there in total disbelief. Her pastor stood before the church and proudly introduced his brother as the guest preacher and thanked him for coming to share with their church for the past four years. Pastor Henderson asked the church to give him a grand welcome and the entire church stood to their feet and began to clap their hands as pastor's brother, Mr. Leprechaun himself, made his way to the pulpit. Victoria thought surely this had to be a look-alike. She had heard people say time and time again that we all have a twin somewhere in the world. She was certain this man must have been a Carl Jackson look-alike. There was no way Carl Jackson was anybody's pastor, nor was he any kind of preacher. The Carl Jackson she knew was a high profile, under-the-radar PIMP. He made a living selling sex and pimping women. There is no way in the world he could be called a preacher.

Victoria stood in total amazement and nearly turned white when the preacher's voice hit the airwaves. As soon as he said, "Praise the Lord, church," Victoria fell in her seat with her mouth wide open because she knew the leprechaun was in the pulpit. This man wasn't dressed in a green suit, but she knew he was her leprechaun. She had never heard him say one word about God the entire time that she had known him, but his voice was one she would never forget. Not only did he look like her pimp, but he certainly sounded like him. This could not be! From that moment on, Victoria did not hear one word he said. She sat in church like a ghost with visions of her horrible past dancing in her head. The leprechaun, as she knew him, was definitely somebody's preacher.

Victoria may not have known him as a preacher, but her pimp was preaching the church crazy. People were high-fiving each other, dancing in the aisles, and crying and screaming! Everyone had said he was a great preacher and it was evident that he really was, but Victoria just couldn't believe it. The man she knew didn't work to save lives; he worked to destroy them. The man she knew didn't pray for people; he preyed on people. The man she knew didn't work for God; he thought he was God. Victoria could not handle this and there was no way in the world she could listen to one word he had to say. Victoria grabbed her purse and left in total disbelief and disgust.

The parking lot ministry workers were out on the lot awaiting church dismissal. There were many people at church, cars were lined up along the perimeter of the highway, and Victoria had completely forgotten where she parked her car. "How could you even think of leaving with a great preacher like that in the pulpit?" Bro. Thomas, one of the parking lot attendants, said to Victoria as she stopped to survey the parking lot trying to remember where she had parked her car.

Victoria wanted to give Bro. Thomas the low down on the great Rev. Carl Jackson, but instead, she simply said her mother needed her help for the family reunion and she was headed there to finish preparations before everyone arrived. Victoria asked the jovial Bro. Thomas if he was going to join them and Bro. Thomas, having watched Victoria grow up over the years, boasted about what a smart young lady Victoria was. "I know your parents are proud of you," he exclaimed. Victoria silently wondered how proud they would be if they knew who their daughter really was and who this great preacher really was! Bro. Thomas told Victoria to hop on the golf cart and he would take her straight to her car.

Sitting on the edge of the bed in her old bedroom at her parent's house again, Victoria felt this was definitely a déjà vu moment. She knew she had been in this place in her life before and she sat wondering how in the world she allowed her life to get off track before leaving Atlanta. And now, before getting dressed to go to the hall, she found herself back in the same position and wondered how in the world her life ended up looking like a Sunday afternoon Lifetime movie. This is definitely not how Victoria desired to live her life. It appeared that she found herself running dead into her ugly secrets at every turn she made. She never would have believed that she would run into her old clients at church, and she certainly never dreamed that she would have gone to church to find her pimp in the pulpit preaching! Victoria prayed, and this time she asked the Lord to give her strength to confront the secrets of her past. She was sick of lying to her parents, her family, her friends, her church members and especially God. This madness had to come to an immediate halt. Victoria made up her mind that she would sit her parents down and tell them the truth after the reunion, but for now, she would make sure everything was picture perfect for her mother's family reunion. Victoria got dressed and made a mad dash to the hall to make sure everything was in place.

Mother Stevens arrived at the hall and all she could do was smile. Victoria had everything together: the DJ had the hall jumping, the tables were nicely decorated, the children ran straight outside to play games and jump in the moonwalk, and the ladies who were helping to serve were all wearing black and turquoise aprons to match the decor. Victoria was elated that she had done everything to make her mother happy. She gave her mom one of the matching aprons and told her she wanted to make sure this was one of the happiest days of her life. She walked her mom around to make sure that everything was just as she wanted it. Mother Stevens was overjoyed at all the hard work Victoria had put into the family reunion.

Family members were quickly arriving. In the midst of kissing and hugging everyone she passed, Mother Stevens informed Victoria that she had invited the pastor, his family, and the guest preacher from Atlanta to have dinner with them. "They are going to be here within the next thirty to forty-five minutes. Could you please make sure they are seated at one of the reserved tables in the front?" her mother said. For the third time, Victoria felt like she had been hit by a meteor falling from the sky. Did her mother just say she invited the pastor and his Leprechaun preaching brother to the family reunion? Now that was just a little too close for comfort. How in the world was Victoria going to come face-to-face with Mr. Carl Jackson in front of all these people?

Victoria wanted to run away and hide. What in the world was she going to do? She needed a plan and she needed one quick. She thought about hiding out in the kitchen, remaining outside with the kids, or maybe even hiding inside of the moonwalk; she just needed a safe place. As soon as Victoria tried to go outside to put her thinking cap on, her mother called for her. Mother Stevens wanted Victoria to check the food table and to place someone in charge of preparing plates for their special guests. Her plan to hideaway had been thwarted by hostess duties. Victoria made her way back to the kitchen and decided that would be the best place to hide. She could see everything from the kitchen area, be available to give any directions, and keep her eyes on the Leprechaun to make sure they did not cross paths.

Once in the kitchen, Victoria took a deep breath, said a prayer asking God to help her get past this awkward moment, and poured herself a cup of coffee to help calm her nerves. The cup of coffee and the constant demands of the guests kept Victoria so busy that within the next twenty minutes the fear of crossing paths with the Leprechaun totally escaped her mind. Rushing to fulfill Vanessa's request for more green beans on the buffet line, Victoria walked out of the kitchen and came face to face with the man she had spent the last year running from: her PIMP – Mr. Leprechaun – the CEO of Global Enterprises – Pastor/Preacher - the Mr. Carl Jackson.

Victoria, for over a year now, had often wondered what this moment would feel like. Little did she know that this moment would actually feel like splattered green bean juice all over her legs. The pan of green beans she was carrying to refill the buffet table ended up on the floor and all over her legs. There, before Victoria, stood a host of family and friends rushing to both clean up the green bean mess and to greet the pastor and his family. Finally, at the moment of truth, Victoria felt like she had fallen into a fox hole with no way out.

Victoria wanted to run and hide. She didn't know whether to force a false introduction or ask Mr. Jackson what in God's name was he doing standing in any pulpit. Oddly enough, it appeared that Mr. Leprechaun/Pastor was also at a loss for words. The last thing any pimp wants to do is lose his bread winner, especially the bread-winning woman his heart is tied to. She remembered him bragging about how he would hunt his girls down and how he would hurt them if they ever tried to leave him for years. Victoria's run from fear had just come to an end. To make matters worse, while everyone was trying to clean up the green bean juice, Mother Stevens stopped to introduce Pastor Jackson to her wonderful daughter, Victoria.

Mother Stevens told Pastor Jackson that Victoria had recently moved home from Atlanta and how she really wished Victoria had met him while she was living in Atlanta. Just as Victoria did not know what to say, Mr. Jackson did not know what to say. Victoria didn't know if Carl would just play it off or if he had some of his goons waiting to snatch her at a moment's notice. Carl gave Victoria the normal church folk greeting hug as Mother Stevens worked her way down the line making sure everyone was formally introduced. Mother Stevens was just about done introducing everyone who came with her pastor when she approached Attorney Nigel Albert and the young lady standing behind him. Mother Stevens gave Nigel another hug as he introduced his wife to her. Amazed by this news, Mother Stevens gave the Alberts another huge hug and told them how she and her husband, James, longed to meet Victoria's Atlanta friends. Victoria could have shriveled up and died on the spot.

Curious, Mother Stevens continuously inquired about the friendship Victoria and Nigel had and repeatedly asked where did they meet. Everyone's silence seemed to have irritated Mother Stevens all the more because she continued to ask how they knew each other. Before anyone could answer, Pastor began joking about how everyone in the entire city of Atlanta knew Nigel Albert because he was such a high profile attorney. Victoria laughed it off and asked that everyone make themselves comfortable until the servers brought their food out. Victoria and Carl exchanged eye contact while Victoria worked to help the ladies serve their guests. Mother Stevens later overheard Mrs. Albert asking Victoria how she had been doing and just how long she planned to keep all of this a secret from everyone. What? Mother Stevens overheard and wondered what secret Mrs. Albert was talking about. Trying real hard to keep it together, Victoria kept her cool and continued to cut the prize-winning cake her family had won as Family of the Year. Mother Stevens' motherly intuition kicked in and she knew something just wasn't right so she stopped and asked Victoria if everything was okay. Victoria assured her mother that everything was fine. They had plenty of food and everything was under control.

Victoria was handling the situation just fine until Mrs. Albert approached her for another piece of cake.

Mrs. Albert walked up to the cake table to return the piece of cake that she had been given and told Victoria, "Ugh, Ms. Victoria! You know I only eat the end piece."

Overhearing those words, Mother Stevens knew something was going on. She turned around, looked at Mrs. Albert and said, "Now just how would she know that? Okay, ladies, no more secrets. You obviously know one another. What's really going on?"

Victoria's dad and a few other men from the church entered in the midst of their conversation. Mother Stevens called him over to the front to meet everyone. Mrs. Albert also experienced an I- have-just-been-hit-by-a- meteor-falling-from-the-sky moment. Before she even realized it, Mrs. Albert screamed, "Oh, my God! Are you Vicky's dad?"

Mother Stevens said, "Well, yes! This is my husband, James. You know my James?" she inquired. *How* do you know James?" Mother Stevens abruptly turned and asked her husband, "Honey, do you know this young lady?" The lack of response from anyone really upset Mother Stevens and she was beginning to lose her cool. She looked at Victoria and asked her again how would she know that this woman only ate the end piece of cake? Mr. Stevens knew his wife very well and knew that she would not stop asking questions until she got the answers she sought.

Mr. Stevens asked his wife to take a seat assuring her he would explain everything. He began by saying, "I knew my ugly secret would catch up with me one day; I just had no idea it would be today." Mr. Stevens asked his daughter to also take a seat. He admitted, "Yes, I know this young lady."

Mr. Stevens said, "Now, Vivian, you know things between us have been really dry for quite some time. We barely say two words to one another, and on top of that, all of your attention is centered on trying to keep up with Victoria or what's going on at the church. We haven't even touched each other in God knows when, and frankly, I got tired of begging for your attention."

Mr. Stevens apologized to his wife and said, "For the past seven years, I have been meeting women every time I go to Atlanta for my business meetings. A while back, Justin mentioned that his brother Carl had a little business on the side pushing girls. He said Carl kept everything low profile and real professional and if I wanted him to make the contact he could hook me up."

Mr. Stevens confessed his dirty little secret to his wife

right there at the very front table of the family reunion. "During my last visit to Atlanta, I told Justin to ask Carl for his best girl. He said it would cost me more, but he would send his best girl, Vicky, to meet me and I agreed. My meeting actually ran over that day and I arrived at the hotel a little late. I had Justin contact Carl and inform him that I would be running a little late and he stated that it was no problem. While awaiting my arrival, Vicky decided to have lunch with another one of Carl's girls in the hotel restaurant. I was instructed to text Carl the room number once I checked in. After I checked into the hotel, I texted Carl as instructed and Samantha arrived shortly thereafter. Samantha informed me that Vicky would not be joining me, but that she would. Samantha informed me that something came up and Vicky could not make it but she promised that I would not be disappointed."

And he wasn't. James agreed not to mention the change to Carl at all. It was during their conversation that James confessed to Samantha that he had peeked into the hotel restaurant to get a glimpse of her before he went up to the room. He told Samantha that he had gotten a look at her and hoped she was Vicky because the other young lady reminded him of his daughter. He shared with her that his daughter had moved to Atlanta and he missed her terribly. Samantha consoled James that night while sitting on the side of the hotel bed. Somehow, their sexual encounter turned into a counseling session for both of them. Samantha realized selling her body for money was not the life for her, and James decided to devote himself to working on his marriage. They both agreed to make changes in their lives. Little did they know they would run into each other at a church function in Dallas, Texas.

Now Mother Stevens was definitely having an I-have-just-been-hit-by-a- meteor-falling-from-the-sky moment. She could not believe what her husband had told her. Mother Stevens said, "Wait. Let me get this straight. You discussed your sexual loneliness with our Pastor, Rev. Justin Henderson, and Pastor Henderson, in turn, told you to contact his brother, the guest preacher for our Family & Friends Day service, Pastor Carl Jackson, and he would hook you up with one of the girls he pimps on the side while he tells the world to live for Jesus? And this beautiful young woman, Samantha, just happens to be the woman he hooked you up with?" Mother Stevens sarcastically asked, "Did I get it right?"

James replied, "Unfortunately, you are right."

By now nearly everyone attending the family reunion dinner was glued in on the action that was taking place with the Stevens family. Mother Stevens could not believe what she had just heard, and neither could Victoria! Victoria hated to see the pain her mother was in and knew that her dirty little secret would not make things better, but she knew the time had come for her to get everything out in the open.

It was a good thing everyone was seated because Victoria knew that her confession was about to knock everyone down. She grabbed her parents by their hands as she began to reveal her past. Victoria began by saying, "Wow! We really do live in a small world. Okay, here goes."

She looked at her father and said, "Daddy, I am Vicky. I am the Vicky that Carl scheduled you to see on that day. I don't know how I got myself into this crazy world, but I did!"

Victoria tried her best to explain everything to her parents. "I left home because the two of you were driving me crazy. The cost of living is extremely high in Atlanta, and I had a hard time making ends meet. I had a job teaching but had to take on a part-time job working at the grocery store to pay my bills. I hated it, but anything was better than coming home to live with you two. I met Carl Jackson one day while working at the grocery store. He came through my checkout line dressed in a lime green suit looking like a leprechaun and offered me a job. At the time, I had no idea he was a pimp and certainly didn't know anything about him being a preacher, but I called him, and the rest is history. I began selling my body for him. I made a lot of money selling my body and showing men—rich, married men—a real good time."

Victoria took a deep breath then continued. "During this time, Carl and I fell in love. Yes, I made a lot of money, lived in a nice place, drove an expensive car, and owned every name brand clothing you could think of, but because of my dirty little secret, I lost my family and my values. Carl only had a few girls who worked for him, and Samantha was the only one who would even talk to me. The rest of the girls hated me because I got his best clients, and I was his woman. Samantha was my only friend. We confided in one another, but it looks like even as friends, we kept secrets from each other. Business was booming in my life, but Samantha had a hard time finding that one man who would give her the world. She longed for a man in her life and in my life I actually had two. My life was centered on Carl, but Nigel was a great friend."

Victoria glanced in Nigel's direction. "Yes, I used to be the call-girl for Atlanta's number-one prosecuting attorney, Nigel Albert. The funny thing is, Nigel and I only had intercourse once. After that one time, he told me he really enjoyed my company, and that he no longer wanted to pay women for sex. He desired to find someone to love and marry. Nigel and I became the best of friends. He and I spent a lot of time together each week. He had standing appointments, and he gave me a lot of money just to have someone to talk to. We spent our evenings talking, shopping, going out for coffee, and just encouraging one another. Over time, I got to know Nigel very well. Although I was Carl's woman, I was really in love with Nigel. Matter of fact, the day you saw us in the hotel restaurant, Samantha and I were having lunch to discuss our way out of the business. Just before lunch, I talked her into taking my next appointment so I could be with Nigel later that night. Samantha shared with me that she had finally met her Prince Charming, and she wanted more than anything to be married to the man of her dreams. Little did I know that her Prince Charming was my best friend, the man I really loved, Nigel Albert."

Victoria paused before continuing. "Samantha was Nigel's girl before I came into the business. Until now, I had no idea the two of them were still seeing one another. The day we met for lunch, we confided in each other that we wanted to get out of the call-girl lifestyle altogether. Our lives were crazy, but both Samantha and I were afraid of Carl and knew he would not let us just walk away from Global

Enterprises. Had Samantha not taken my next appointment, it would have been your own daughter arriving in your hotel room to sex you down."

Victoria looked away embarrassed before continuing. "Instead, over a cup of coffee, Nigel shared his desire for a wife. He confessed that he had met a woman, and he felt that she was the one. I thought he was talking about me until he told me how he wanted me to meet her. It was that night that I realized just how much I loved him. I was Carl Jackson's woman, but I was in love with Nigel Albert. I lied to Nigel, Carl, and myself because I honestly wanted more than friendship from Nigel. After realizing I was not the woman Nigel wanted, I couldn't take it another day. I had to leave that night. I could never face seeing Nigel with another woman; my love for him would not allow it."

Closing her eyes tight to hold back unwanted tears, Victoria continued, "I went back to my beautiful penthouse apartment that Carl paid for, and realized my heart was tied to another man—a man that made his living sharing pieces of my body with other men and contracting me out for sexual favors to deepen his pockets. This secret lifestyle was killing me, and to discover the man I loved didn't want me was entirely too much for me to deal with. I can recall having to deal with it all like it was yesterday. My mind was on overload, so I sat on the balcony trying to clear my head. The sound of the water trickling from the waterfall on my beautiful balcony caused me to fall fast asleep and about two hours later, I was awakened to a phone call from you, Mom."

Mother Stevens managed a forced faint smile as her eyes connected with her daughter's. "That night you called and encouraged me to trust the plan that God had for my life. You told me that no man would take care of me like God would; it was then that I looked at the men in my life and knew I had it all wrong. I had trusted other men to take care of me, and it was on that night that I realized I already had the one man that I needed in my life, and that was God."

Victoria felt relief coming over her as she disclosed her past secret.

"I realized I had been trying so hard to do things my way, but my way had led me straight to a life of destruction. I knew deep down in my heart that my choice of lifestyles was not what God had intended for my life. I wanted to make it big in life, but there was nothing big about my lifestyle. The only big thing was a dirty secret that led to lies, a broken heart, damaged emotions, low self-esteem, lost values, and pain. I knew that this so-called luxurious call-girl life style was not what God had planned for me. So I boxed up everything I owned, rented a U-Haul, and ran from my past. I cut off all communication with everyone from my past. I left my dirty little secrets in Atlanta and came back to Dallas. I thought all of this was behind me, but here, all in one day, the skeletons of my past have built a graveyard right here in front of God, my family, and my church family. So much for Family of the Year!"

By now, Mother Stevens' head was on the table with her hands over her ears. Her Dad was flabbergasted to discover that his Victoria and Samantha's Vicky were both one and the same. From the looks of things Victoria wasn't the only sister with a secret:

- Victoria's father had been sneaking around with women for quite some time.

- Their pastor, Rev. Justin Henderson, was sneaking around. He knew his brother was a pimp and encouraged the men of the church to utilize his business. In fact, several men of the congregation confessed that they too had used the brother's services. Rev. Henderson never dreamed that one of his members would be one of his brother's working girls.

- Pastor/Preacher/Pimp/Lennie look-alike Carl Jackson's was a Pastor/preacher who pimped women on the side and fell in love with Victoria.

- Attorney, Nigel Albert, had been Carl Jackson's number one client until he slipped off and married one of his girls behind his back. Nigel was tired of hiding and accepted the invitation to attend the church services with plans to tell Carl that he and Samantha were now married.

Mother Stevens' dream of hosting a family reunion to reunite the family had quickly turned out to be her worst nightmare. Everyone had a secret that they were hiding that affected the lives of others to some degree. Tears were flowing, and it was evident their lives had been forever changed. It was one church service that brought them all together, but their secret lies had them all entangled in a web of guilt and shame. Justin knew his brother, Carl, was pimping women but had no idea that his brother would be pimping James' (his golfing buddy/church member's) daughter (Victoria), nor did he ever imagine that his brother would one day, in turn, schedule his best friend's own daughter as his woman of pleasure. In a moment's notice, all of the guilty parties began arguing over what they did not know about one another and the awful secrets they kept from each other. Immediately, everyone began to beat up on the preaching brothers for their hidden secrets and lies when Victoria yelled, "Stop it! We are all guilty! Yeah, they are Men of God, but we are all Children of God, and we are all wrong for the choices we have made. I knew better but didn't do better."

* * * * *

I know you are probably reading this chapter thinking how stupid can Victoria be? You are probably wondering if she had lost her mind. I am certain you want to jump inside this chapter and shake her until she comes to her senses, but before you write Victoria off, take a moment and do a personal inventory of your own life. I am willing to bet that much like Victoria, you have messed up a time or two. Maybe you did not meet a pimp in a lime green suit and give into a life of prostitution, but if you are honest, you will admit that something or someone has been a pimp in your life. I know you are reading and thinking to yourself, "Pimped? Oh, NO, not me!" Oh, YES, you! Allow me to prove to you that I am right:

If your $395 designer bag only has $30.00 in it, you have been PIMPED! If the outfit you wore to church last Easter Sunday cost more than what you have saved in the bank, you have been PIMPED! If you wore your daughter's dress to your class reunion, you have been PIMPED! If you are taking pills to go to sleep and pills to stay awake, you have been PIMPED! If your name is Jane and your lover's name is Janice, you have been PIMPED! If you are dating a married man waiting for him to leave his wife, you have been PIMPED! If you are smoking a little weed every now and then to calm your nerves, you have been PIMPED! If you are purchasing bootleg CD's and DVD's from the man standing outside the beauty salon, you have been PIMPED! If your telephone bill is in your three-year-old baby's name, you have been PIMPED! And for my male counterparts that may have this publication in hand, I dare not leave you out: If your name is Jim and your lover's name is James, you too, have been PIMPED! PIMPED! PIMPED! PIMPED!

The enemy is PIMPING the lives of believers from all walks of life, including you and me. Don't be surprised, he is on his job. Nestled away in the New Testament pages of Holy Writ, 1 Peter 5:8, the author pens, "Be alert and of sober mind. Your enemy the devil prowls around like a roaring lion looking for someone to devour."

Know this: Your enemy may not have on a lime green suit, but you can best believe he has taken you as his personal property and brought corruption to your future and your destiny. No matter what the enemy has used as a tool to trap you, you don't have to remain in the pit he has placed you in. Examine yourself and make that decision to change — a change that says I am tired of being trapped in the enemy's pit and come hell or high water, I will embrace all that God has ordained for my life.

Chapter 10
Seeking A Way Out

Many people desire to change. Many see the need to change. Change is inevitable. The will to change is an objective of many. The knowledge to produce a change is a challenge of many. When it comes to change, words of wisdom have been offered by some of the greatest authors on the universe:

British orator, author, and Prime Minister during World War II, Winston Churchill said, *"There is nothing wrong with change, if it is in the right direction."*

Indian philosopher, internationally esteemed for his doctrine of nonviolent protest, Mahatma Gandhi said, *"Be the change you want to see in the world."*

Internationally respected leadership expert, speaker, and author John Maxwell said, *"As you begin changing your thinking, start immediately to change your behavior. Begin to act the part of the person you would like to become. Take action on your behavior. Too many people want to feel, then take action. This never works."*

President John Fitzgerald Kennedy, the 35th President of the United States of America said, *"Change is the law of life. And those who look only to the past or present are certain to miss the future."*

President Barack Obama, the 44th President of the United States of America, who is also the first African-American President said, *"Change will not come if we wait for some other person or some other time. We are the ones we've been waiting for. We are the change that we seek."*

And I am certain that you can recite from memory the inspirational words of American theologian Reinhold Niebuhr's "Prayer of Serenity." Either noted on a refrigerator magnet, a plaque on the wall in your office, or the ribbon bookmark in your Bible are the words, *"God grant me the serenity to accept the things I cannot change, the courage to change the things I can, and the wisdom to know the difference."*

Although I highly respect the words of wisdom offered by all of the aforementioned authors, I am quite partial to the wisdom afforded in Niebuhr's prayer. Niebuhr makes his request for change to God our Father. There is no better place to start over than starting over with God.

As we travel this journey called life, we will encounter pitfalls, setbacks, discouragement, disappointments, bad decisions, failures, sickness, disease, bad credit, no credit, and let's not forget our back stabbing two-faced fake friends. But no matter where you may find yourself, know that our God is able to change your situation. Please allow me to encourage you not to be fathomed by the reflection you see in the mirror, but to trust what you know about God. Your present situation is not your final outcome.

The Bible speaks of many who have fallen by the wayside, but our God provided them the blessing of ANOTHER chance. Noah was a drunkard; King David was guilty of murder and adultery; Rahab was a whore; and Moses was a murderer. In spite of the bad decisions they made, God still blessed them. The woman with the issue of blood stayed sick for twelve long years, but she got healed. Jairus' daughter died, but Jesus resurrected her. Shadrach, Meshach, and Abednego were thrown into a fiery furnace, but they were not burned. The children of Israel stumbled into a situation with the Red Sea in front of them and

Pharaoh and his army behind them, but God provided them a cement sidewalk to safety. I am of the belief that if God did it for them, He will do the same thing for both you and me when we learn to trust God and the will He has for our lives. We must believe that it shall come to pass.

Nestled away in the Old Testament, the prophet Jeremiah writes a letter to the captives of Babylon. In the midst of their captivity, he seeks to encourage them. He encourages them to make the best of their present situation. Yes, it's been seventy years, but Jeremiah reminds them that God will keep His promise. God promised to visit them in the midst of it all, grant them mercy, and put an end to their madness. *"For thus saith the LORD, That after seventy years be accomplished at Babylon I will visit you, and perform my good word toward you, in causing you to return to this place. For I know the thoughts that I think toward you, saith the LORD, thoughts of peace, and not of evil, to give you an expected end"* (Jeremiah 29:10-11, KJV).

Victoria's decision to become involved in the life of prostitution was not the best decision she could have made. As a matter of fact, it was dumb and stupid. But I can't talk about her without looking in the mirror myself. I dare you to go take a look in the mirror. Be careful, you just may not like what you see. I, too, have made a few bad decisions in my life. I did not get PIMPED by a man in a lime green suit, but I have been PIMPED by men who told me they loved me, PIMPED by the lust for famous name brand handbags, PIMPED by the demon of bad credit, PIMPED by the desire to please everyone and make everyone else happy, and PIMPED by the pain of outward beauty and low inner self-esteem. In a strong desire to heal myself, I found that the words Jeremiah penned comforted the madness that engulfed my life. Honestly, I don't recall when it happened, but somehow the enemy tiptoed into my life, snatched my dreams and desires, and had the audacity to hold them hostage.

Finally, the day came when I realized that God had more for my life, and His will for my life was not determined by what others thought about me. I began to seek God through fasting, praying, and speaking the words of Jeremiah into my life! Instead of having a pity party, I was determined to fight for what the enemy stole from me. You can either allow the enemy to keep your destiny, or you can demand that he release it. If you are like me, you will fight for what belongs to you. How do you fight for a change? What do you do to seek God's will for your life? What's the secret to my change? I shared the secret to my change with Victoria, and I want to share it with you.

Chapter 11
I Have the Secret

Shh! Don't tell anyone! Have you ever shared a secret with someone and they told it? Or were you the one to tell it? When we think of a secret, we normally think of hot juicy gossip that someone has shared with us. You know the conversations that start with the words, "Shh! Don't tell anyone! Make sure you keep this a secret!" Well, I have a secret I want to share with you. I know you are glued into this chapter like it's the latest episode of "The Real Housewives of Atlanta"!

'Secret' is defined by Webster's Dictionary to mean something taken to be specific or the key to a desired end. Numerous publications have been produced to share the many secrets to successful living, financial freedom, loving yourself, staying married, raising smart kids, staying skinny, teen power, and the list goes on. I am certain there is a book written to give you a successful outline to enhance your daily living on any subject you can think of. The secrets I desire to share with you are straight from what I consider to be the best book which offers words of wisdom for successful living, The Holy Bible.

The Old Testament book of Jeremiah reminds us that the Lord promises to return and perform His "good" word: (*For thus saith the LORD, That after seventy years be accomplished at Babylon I will visit you, and perform my good word toward you, in causing you to return to this place. Jeremiah 29:10 KJV).* The word 'good' in its original Hebrew translation is [*towb* /*tobe*] defined as good, pleasant, or agreeable. And the 'word' [*dabar*/ *daw-bar*] means to speak, declare, converse, command, promise, warn, or threaten. The Lord promises that even after experiencing seventy years of defeat, pain, and agony He will heal, deliver, and set the captives free.

I don't know if you are shouting yet, but the promise the Lord made to the people in Babylon is still in effect. Thank You, Jesus! No matter what your situation may look like, when you entrust it to God, He will come through. As long as our God, the One who knows the future, has His hands on anything that concerns His children, He will work it out. This does not mean that we will not have to endure pain, suffering, or hardship; but what we do know is that

God will see us through to a glorious conclusion. Your victory starts with His Word. The Lord's Word is powerful! Hebrews 4:12 (KJV) says, "For the word of God is alive and active. Sharper than any double-edged sword, it penetrates even to dividing soul and spirit, joints and marrow; it judges the thoughts and attitudes of the heart." Psalm 119:105 (KJV) says, "Your word is a lamp for my feet, a light on my path."

Let me share this juicy secret with you. Now this you really can't tell anyone. One evening while traveling with my husband, he got turned around and made a wrong turn. As I proceeded to correct him, he informed me that he knew where he was going. For some reason, men hate asking for directions. I could not stand it that he did not want my help, so I suggested that he use the navigation system installed in our vehicle. Finally, he requested assistance, and we were on our way. A few miles later, my husband stated that nothing looked familiar, and we had to be heading in the wrong direction. We telephoned the operator again. The operator made note of our position and informed my husband that we were traveling in the right direction. The operator instructed my husband to continue to follow the planned route.

Convinced that the directions were wrong, my husband dialed the operator for the third time to inform her that her directions must have been wrong, and the we were heading the wrong way. The representative became agitated with my husband and sternly said, "Mr. Albert, you are headed in the right direction." She then said, "I apologize, sir, but we can only give you the directions, we cannot make you follow them."

WOW! It was the operator's voice but definitely a message from God. I really wanted to say, "I told you so!" But the Lord wouldn't let me. He had a greater lesson for me to learn. The Lord has provided each one of us with His words of promise. His plan for our lives is made available to each one of us, but we must learn to follow His guidance. It is imperative that we learn to follow the plan that God has prepared for our lives.

Victoria found it hard to follow the plan that the Lord had for her life and so did I. Have you ever been guilty of doing things your own way? Have you ever known better, but simply didn't do better? Did you see the sign telling you that that tall, dark, and handsome one wasn't the one, but you got involved anyway? Did you write the check knowing that your account was already in the negative? The truth is, we have all had experiences in our lives where we did just what we were big and bad enough to do, choosing not to follow the words of the Lord. Although it was the voice of the navigation system representative speaking, I heard the voice of God reminding me that He has provided a plan for my life, and I must learn to follow His plan. Our God loves us enough to give us His Word, but He can't make us take Him at His Word! We have to learn to trust Him! You have the secret! You have God's promises! You have His Word!

What's Your Secret?
Take a moment and identify the secrets in your life that you need to change. Large or small, our God is the only One who can fix your situation. Trust God enough and take Him at His Word!

_____

_____

_____

_____

_____

_____

_____

_____

_____

_____

_____

_____

_____

Secrets from our Savior

"Give your entire attention to what God is doing right now, and don't get worked up about what may or may not happen tomorrow. God will help you deal with whatever hard things come up when the time comes." – Matthew 6:34, MSG

"Open your mouth and taste, open your eyes and see — how good God is. Blessed are you who run to him. Worship God if you want the best; worship opens doors to all his goodness. Young lions on the prowl get hungry, but God-seekers are full of God" – Psalm 34:8-10, MSG

"Don't bargain with God. Be direct. Ask for what you need. This isn't a cat-and-mouse, hide-and-seek game we're in. If your child asks for bread, do you trick him with sawdust? If he asks for fish, do you scare him with a live snake on his plate? As bad as you are, you wouldn't think of such a thing. You're at least decent to your own children. So don't you think the God who conceived you in love will be even better?" – Matthew 7:7-11, MSG

"So be content with who you are, and don't put on airs. God's strong hand is on you; he'll promote you at the right time. Live carefree before God; he is most careful with you" - I Peter 5:6-7, MSG

"The earlier revelation was intended simply to get us ready for the Messiah, who then puts everything right

for those who trust him to do it. Moses wrote that anyone who insists on using the law code to live right before God soon discovers it's not so easy—every detail of life regulated by fine print! But trusting God to shape the right living in us is a different story—no precarious climb up to heaven to recruit the Messiah, no dangerous descent into hell to rescue the Messiah. So what exactly was Moses saying? The word that saves is right here, as near as the tongue in your mouth, as close as the heart in your chest. It's the word of faith that welcomes God to go to work and set things right for us. This is the core of our preaching. Say the welcoming word to God—'Jesus is my Master'— embracing, body and soul, God's work of doing in us what he did in raising Jesus from the dead. That's it. You're not 'doing' anything; you're simply calling out to God, trusting him to do it for you. That's salvation. With your whole being you embrace God setting things right, and then you say it, right out loud: 'God has set everything right between him and me!' – Romans 10:4-10, MSG

"God will lavish you with good things: children from your womb, offspring from your animals, and crops from your land, the land that God promised your ancestors that he would give you. God will throw open the doors of his sky vaults and pour rain on your land on schedule and bless the work you take in hand. You will lend to many nations but you yourself won't have to take out a loan. God will make you the head, not the tail; you'll always be the top dog, never the bottom dog, as you obediently listen to and

diligently keep the commands of God, your God, that I am commanding you today. Don't swerve an inch to the right or left from the words that I command you today by going off following and worshiping other gods." - Deuteronomy 28:11-14, MSG

Sisters' Authority

Our God is able! Take authority over your situation and apply the Word of God to it. Take a moment and write a prayer concerning your above situations that includes the power of God's Word. Speak life!

Here's an example:

Lord, my body needs healing. There are days I feel that the pain is totally unbearable. I feel like giving up, but, Lord, You said if I would call upon Your name, You would come and see about me. Lord, You promised that I could just cast all of my cares upon You for You care for me. You said if I would ask anything in Your name You would do it, and, Lord, I am asking for You to heal my body. I know You can and I know You will! Lord, I am taking You at Your Word, for no weapon formed against me shall prosper. In the name of Jesus I pray. Amen.

_____

_____

_____

_____

_____

_____

Chapter 12

I Know the Secret

We all have at least one 'know-it-all' friend. You know this person; no matter what you are talking about, this person has the answer to everything, and if the truth be told, this person doesn't know it all, they just think they do. It is always difficult to hold a conversation with know-it-alls, because according to them they have the answers to fix every part of your life. If you are sick, they have a cure. If you are broke, they know the next get rich quick scheme to make you wealthy. If you are lonely, they know the perfect person to hook you up with. If you want to shop, they know where to get the best bargains. If you mention you want to go on vacation, you should go where they went on vacation because they know just the place to send you, and they know everybody there.

Let me be honest: know-it-alls get on my nerves. Know-it-alls have already been there and they have already tried that; they know the ins and outs of the situation and know-it-alls know everybody. You can never get a word in when talking to a know-it-all. A know-it-all will cut you off in conversation to tell you what they already know when they really don't know anything about you and the situation you may be dealing with. Know-it-alls will make you think they know the answers to your problems and they will tell you just how you should respond to others and the massive pitfalls of life. Generally, these folks have issues of their own and think they know what others should do, but live lives that are falling apart. I have never understood how people can give such sound advice to others, yet, when you peep into their lives, everything is torn up from the floor up.

People are always eager to tell you what to do to fix your life, but that does not mean that it is the right thing for you to do. When you are faced with situations, many will give their opinions and advice, even though they have never walked in your shoes. We are often given advice by others who have no idea what God has planned for our lives. The path that the Lord has orchestrated for your life is not the same path that He has for someone else's life. Others often share their thoughts and ideas on how to live your life when they have no idea where the Lord is taking you. It's very hard to tell me how to get to Hollywood Boulevard if you have never been there yourself. Maybe you can give me directions to Hollywood

Boulevard, but your directions may only get me to Hollywood Boulevard in Beaumont, Texas, when I actually need directions to get to Hollywood Boulevard in Los Angeles, California. And if you have never been there, you can't help me. In other words, a person who has never been where you are going can't offer you the directions you need. Everyone does not have the same goal, dream, or desire.

What we fail to remember is that the Lord has already prepared His plan and purpose for our lives. Our God is the only One we should consult when we are going through things in life. It's a waste of time, energy, and tears to try to do what others are doing, to try to be like other people, to live by the opinions of others, and to listen to know-it-alls who have no clue as to what the Lord has ordained for your life. What God has planned has been tailor-made with only you in mind. The path that He has prepared for someone else may look easier, but it's not what God has planned for you. His plan may take you longer to get where you are going, the road you have to take may have more pit-falls and road blocks, and the Lord may have you remain at the rest stop for a longer period of time compared to others. You may even have to ride on the feeder road while others travel the highway. But trust me, no matter what it may look like, have confidence in the plan that God has orchestrated for your life. Learn to seek God, listen to His voice, and move at His command.

In the previous chapter, we took a close look at Jeremiah 29:10. Let's proceed to the 11th verse where Jeremiah writes: *"For I know the plans I have for you, declares the LORD, "plans to prosper you and not to harm you, plans to give you hope and a future.* The word 'know' in its original Hebrew translation means to know by experience. In the last chapter, we learned about the power of God's Word. Remember Hebrews 4:12 (KJV) says, "For the word of God is alive and active. Sharper than any double-edged sword, it penetrates even to dividing soul and spirit, joints and marrow; it judges the thoughts and attitudes of the heart." Psalm 119:105 (KJV) promises "Your word is a lamp for my feet, a light on my path."

There is power in God's Word, and as children of God, we have the authority to utilize the power of God's Word. You have to trust what you know about God to heal your situation. When we are faced with the ups and downs of life, we have to trust the same God who fixed it the last time to fix it once again. Don't you know if He did it once, He will do it again? Don't you know if He did it for Mary, He will do it for you. Don't waste time listening to know-it-alls. You don't have to try to figure it out; God has already worked it out. What I find so amazing about God is that He always proves Himself. It is impossible for the know-it-alls in our lives to instruct us on what to do because they have no idea what God has planned for our lives. The God in us is bigger than the whole world against us. In Ephesians 3:20 (KJV) His Word says, *Now to him who is able to do immeasurably more than all we ask or imagine, according to his power that is at work within us.* As believers we must learn to trust what we know about God.

Trust. It's much easier to say that we trust a person than to really trust them. There is something about our human nature that keeps us from trusting one another. I'm not sure if it's the crab mentality, jealousy, or envy, but it's not easy to trust someone. Trust and promise go hand in hand. If you are one to break a promise, then it will be quite difficult for me to place my trust in you. As a society, we make and break promises every day. The world has an overflow of children suffering financially and emotionally because of dead-beat dads who promised to provide for the children they created in the heat of the moment. How did this happen? Broken promises!

Day in and day out, creditors are chasing individuals who signed on the dotted line an agreement to repay the credit that was given to them. Broken promises have forced many parents to teach their children to lie at an early age by instructing them to tell worrying creditors that they are not home just to keep from dealing with their broken promises.

Broken promises are the reason seventy-two year-old grandmothers have their grand-children's sports cars hidden in their garages with hopes that the repo man doesn't swing by to repossess their automobile.

According to statistics, broken promises are the reason the divorce rate is at an all-time high. Husbands and wives who promised to love one another until death do them part, after fourteen years "cannot stand being around each other."

Broken promises make it hard to trust anyone or anything around you. It amazes me how we so freely put our trust in things and opportunities instead of each other. Without even thinking about it, as soon as the state fair comes to town, we find ourselves sitting on the roller coaster grinning and throwing our hands up in the air without any thought as to the safety of the ride. I don't know about you, but there was a time when I would stand in line to ride the most daring ride and never give thought to the last time the ride passed any type of inspection. I know I am not the only one who has snapped the seat belt trusting the ride and its operator for the thrill of a lifetime as I yelled, "Weeeeee!!!!" with my body jerking from left to right.

Without hesitation, we board airplanes trusting our lives 40,000 feet in the air to pilots we never see. Think about it: most of the time you board the plane and never even meet the pilot. It's not until you've been in the air for nearly an hour that he/she even speaks on the intercom: "Welcome to flight 1439, I'm your pilot..." By this time, you are asleep or miss the entire greeting because you are listening to the latest and greatest that you've downloaded on your playlist. Nevertheless, you have entrusted your life into the hands of a total stranger, 40,000 feet in the air. What I find most funny is that we can trust a man or woman to take us 40,000 feet in the air, but we can't or won't trust persons standing three feet in front of us.

While on a cruise vacation in October 2010 with my sister and sistah friends, I fulfilled a lifelong dream to parasail. Our cruise ship arrived safely to Coco Cay, Bahamas, and we embarked on the excursion of a lifetime. I found myself nearly thirty-eight stories high in the air, trusting a tow line with a knot in it to hold me up—a tow line that was manned by two men I had never met. I shall not lie: the knot I witnessed in the tow line made me a little nervous at first, but once we were high in the air, I never gave my safety a second thought. My girlfriend, Natalie, and I were dangling our feet high in the air, giggling, laughing, and talking about how amazing God was.

The Lord must have taken our conversation as a prayer because He covered us with His blood and held the knot in the tow line. Various situations have taught me to trust God and take Him at His Word even when others have failed me! God is so amazing!

Trust issues are nothing new for me. I have been hurt a time or two by people. I have been hurt by men who said they loved me, by women who said they were my friends, and by family members with unreal standards. My trust issues with people made it even harder for me to trust God. I grew up in the church and heard that God would never fail me, but it took a real experience with God on September 11, 2001, for me to learn that He was the One who I could always trust. Like most believers I did trust God, but often believed that He took too long to give me what I wanted, so I would often get in His way and try to fix the situation myself or at least so I thought.

Please don't judge me, I am sure if you are honest, you will admit you have done the exact same thing. Many of you can testify that you, too, have gotten in God's way and messed up your blessings. Individuals have married the wrong person because of a lack of trust in God. Some have even experienced living from paycheck to paycheck because trust in God didn't exist. Had trust in God existed, the outcome of life would be so different. It wasn't until the Lord allowed me to experience failure that I found that God really loves me, and I can trust Him.

For many years, I worked in retail management with the nation's largest, roll-back prices retail chain. Managing a store in this chain required many hours that caused me to be away from my family most of the time. Even my days off were spent on call, worrying about sales, and worrying about the individuals I managed. After giving this chain seven years of my life, I began to seek God asking Him to release me from this job. The money was good, and the benefits were great, but I hated not being home with my children. My husband was forced to be Mr. Mom, and when he was working, my children were being raised by family members and baby-sitters. I was tired of missing so much of their precious adolescent years.

The consideration to leave the company really came at a difficult time. My husband and I were having our first home built and at that time in our lives, I was the financial bread winner. I shared my desire to leave the store with my husband, and we prayed to God asking Him to have His way. In faith, I wrote a letter of resignation to my district manager, and my husband and I told our bank representative of my plans to leave my job. Both of these gentlemen instructed me to keep my job, or we would never become the homeowners of the home we were building. In faith, we prayed and trusted God. The Lord told me to go ahead and leave my job with the store. I had no idea how He would make a way for my family financially. I did like the idea of being a stay-at-home mom but began to become overwhelmed with worry about the family finances, and I surely was not used to having to ask my husband for money to feed my addiction—shoes! Instead of just trusting God with the situation, my worry got the best of me.

Now, remember, I asked the Lord to release me from the job with the store so that I could stay at home with my children. The Lord honored my request, but I had no idea how the Lord would work out our finances. With a great desire to help the Lord out, I began searching for another job, but this time one with fewer hours. A position as a financial adviser for a multinational financial corporation became available and the attractive salary, 8 A.M. – 5 P.M. hours, and weekends off, lured me in. Before I knew it, I was back in the saddle again. Taking the job was the solution to my worry, but honestly, I never consulted the Lord about the job. I prayed for the Lord to help me, but I did this one all on my own.

I was excited about the pay and the weeks of training that I had to take in New York City. I had never been to New York but had always wanted to go. Now I would go on a company paid trip and live in a company paid hotel for nearly a month. What was there that I needed the Lord to figure out? This time, I had everything under control, or at least so I thought. The Lord has a way of proving Himself. Everything I asked God for He supplied, but I still did not trust Him to work everything out.

I was scheduled to be in the World Trade Center Building on September 11, 2001, for training classes. However, after failing the Series 7 Exam, the dates for my training classes were rescheduled for a later time. While awaiting my newly rescheduled travel date, I witnessed the tragedy of 9/11 that changed the mindset of America forever. Had things gone my way, I may have been among the thousands who lost their lives on that day. BUT GOD! Immediately following the attack, the Holy Spirit comforted my spirit with one verse: *"For I know the plans I have for you," declares the Lord, "plans to prosper you and not to harm you, plans to give you hope and a future"* (Jeremiah 29:11).

My trust issues were difficult, but now I know without a shadow of a doubt that the Lord will work it out. I am still living in the home we were told we would not be able to build without my roll-back prices income, and I have purchased enough shoes to open a shoe store of my own. When you trust God, He will make a way. By my own experiences, I can testify that God will take care of you. Our God loves us enough to be true to His promises. God will fix it. Get out of God's way and trust Him because God never fails!

There is one know-it-all that I am so glad I do know, and that is God! It has not been an easy journey for me, but I have come to realize that God has a plan for my life, and I have learned to trust Him. I honestly thought I had it all together and knew exactly what I would do with my life until I realized I had totally forgotten to check with God. Finally, I made one of the best decisions I have ever made, and that was the decision to stop listening to everyone around me and start listening for the voice of God. Listening for the voice of God is a lot easier when we learn to drown out everything around us and tune in to His voice.

The competitive sport of rowing provides a visual illustration that just blows my mind each time I consider it. Imagine eight athletes seated in a boat, facing the stern and using oars to propel the boat forward towards the bow. Also seated inside the boat facing the bow is a man or woman known as the coxswain. Also called the cox, the coxswain is in charge of the crew and gives all the commands and makes all tactical decisions. This person provides motivation and encouragement to the crew, and informs the crew of where they are in relation to other crews and the finish line. The coxswain steers the boat and coordinates the power and rhythm of the rowers by communicating to the crew through a device with speakers called a cox box. I have inserted a photo to help bring this visual to life so you can really get your shout on.

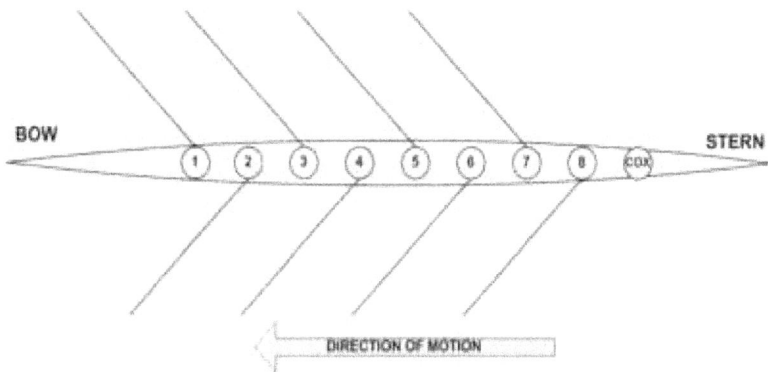

The athletes positioned inside of the boat are working to move the boat forward, but forward is actually what's behind them. The athletes cannot see where they are headed; they depend upon the coxswain to give the correct instructions to reach their destination. When the coxswain commands, "Ready all, row!" they move at his command. This illustration truly blessed my life. The athletes positioned in the boat do not know what is ahead of them; they depend totally on their coxswain to lead them. Wait! Hold your shout; it gets even better! There are several boats all trying to make it to the finish line, and each boat has their own coxswain. The athletes are trained only to respond to the voice of their coxswain.

Winning is achieved by the athletes who have learned to keep their eyes and ears fixed to the coxswain in their boat. The athletes have learned to move only at the command of the voice that is leading them.

Our daily living is so much like the sport of rowing. If we would learn to just listen and trust the voice of God, our very own coxswain, we would win the race. God knows exactly where we are headed, and He knows exactly how to get us across the finish line.

As believers, we must learn to listen and move at the commands the Lord gives us. When the Lord says, "NO, don't marry him!" Then don't marry him! "NO, don't buy that purse!" Then leave it in the store. "NO, leave that married man alone!" Then leave that married man alone. Jesus is our coxswain! Learn to listen to the voice of God and your life will be so much better. I do not know what the Lord has prepared for my life, but I do know He can see the path to get me exactly where He wants me to go. I must learn to keep my eyes on the Lord and listen to His command. I can't worry about what is going on in someone else's boat; I have to stay focused and follow the commands of my coxswain. The voice of God is where I am taking my directions from. Jesus is my coxswain!

I love the Message Bible translation of Proverbs 3:5-6: *"Trust GOD from the bottom of your heart; don't try to figure out everything on your own. Listen for GOD's voice in everything you do, everywhere you go; he's the one who will keep you on track."*

What's Your Secret?

Take a moment and identify the moments in your life where you have heard the voice of God giving you direction. Trust God enough and take Him at His Word!

_____

_____

_____

_____

_____

_____

_____

_____

Secrets from our Savior

"Trust God from the bottom of your heart; don't try to figure out everything on your own. Listen for God's voice in everything you do, everywhere you go; he's the one who will keep you on track. Don't assume that you know it all. Run to God! Run from evil! Your body will glow with health, your very bones will vibrate with life! Honor God with everything you own; give him the first and the best. Your barns will burst, your wine vats will brim over. But don't, dear friend, resent God's discipline; don't sulk under his loving correction. It's the child he loves that God corrects; a father's delight is behind all this."

– Proverbs 3:5-12, MSG

"Pay close attention now: I'm creating new heavens and a new earth. All the earlier troubles, chaos, and pain are things of the past, to be forgotten. Look ahead with joy. Anticipate what I'm creating: I'll create Jerusalem as sheer joy, create my people as pure delight. I'll take joy in Jerusalem, take delight in my people: No more sounds of

weeping in the city, no cries of anguish; No more babies dying in the cradle, or old people who don't enjoy a full lifetime; One-hundredth birthdays will be considered normal—anything less will seem like a cheat. They'll build houses and move in. They'll plant fields and eat what they grow. No more building a house that some outsider takes over, No more planting fields that some enemy confiscates, For my people will be as long-lived as trees, my chosen ones will have satisfaction in their work. They won't work and have nothing come of it, they won't have children snatched out from under them. For they themselves are plantings blessed by God, with their children and grandchildren likewise God-blessed. Before they call out, I'll answer. Before they've finished speaking, I'll have heard. Wolf and lamb will graze the same meadow, lion and ox eat straw from the same trough, but snakes—they'll get a diet of dirt! Neither animal nor human will hurt or kill anywhere on my Holy Mountain, says God." – Isaiah 65:17-25, MSG

"At that time, this song will be sung in the country of Judah: We have a strong city, Salvation City, built and fortified with salvation. Throw wide the gates so good and true people can enter. People with their minds set on you, you keep completely whole, Steady on their feet, because they keep at it and don't quit. Depend on God and keep at it because in the Lord God you have a sure thing. Those who lived high and mighty he knocked off their high horse. He used the city built on the hill as fill for the marshes.

All the exploited and outcast peoples build their lives on the reclaimed land." –Isaiah 26:1-6, MSG

"Even when the way goes through Death Valley, I'm not afraid when you walk at my side. Your trusty shepherd's crook makes me feel secure." –Psalm 23:4, MSG

Sisters' Authority

Our God is able! Take authority over your situation and apply the Word of God to it. Take a moment and write a prayer concerning your above situations that includes the power of God's Word! When you write your prayer repeat the promises the Lord has made to you! Etch the words of God in your heart: *"And Jesus answering saith unto them, Have faith in God. For verily I say unto you, That whosoever shall say unto this mountain, be thou removed, and be thou cast into the sea; and shall not doubt in his heart, but shall believe that those things which he saith shall come to pass; he shall have whatsoever he saith. Therefore I say unto you, What things soever ye desire, when ye pray, believe that ye receive them, and ye shall have them."* –Mark 11:22-24, MSG

Speak life!

Here's an example:

Lord, I Need You! As I look over my life, the people of my past have failed me, and my decisions have not always

been the best. I am tired and in need of a change in my life. Lord, I trust You and need to hear from You. Speak to my present situation and provide me a way of escape. I feel defeated and discouraged, but I know that one word from You will change everything in my life! Speak, Lord! Lord, I need You, and I can't make it without You. Forgive me for relying on others. Your Word promises that You will never leave me nor forsake me. Thank You, Lord, for getting ahead of me and making the crooked pathway in my life straight!

_____

_____

_____

_____

_____

_____

_____

_____

_____

_____

_____

_____

_____

Chapter 13
I Expect The Secret To Be Revealed

Harboring a secret leads one to live a double life. Individuals who attempt to live double lives are never successful and never satisfied with their double lives or their duplicitous selves. Dual lifestyle choices are risky formulas for self-sabotage. It's impossible to receive what God intended for your life if you're living someone else's life. Unfortunately, a search on the internet will reveal that there are millions of Americans living double lives every day. This sad truth is equally common in the lives of both men and women who are believers. It's obvious that having a secret life is not as unusual or abnormal as one may think. The world is filled with Bible-toting, Scripture-quoting men and women who live daily in two separate worlds — worlds that are engulfed with their own lies, and lives overpowered by self-inflicted guilt and shame. As a result, make believe worlds now exist to cover up unbelievable secrets from the people nearest and dearest to their hearts: family members, friends, co-workers, church members, and other believers.

The word 'secret' as defined by *Merriam-Webster*, means to keep from knowledge or view, something hidden. Secrets lead to lives of deception and destruction. The deceiver becomes caught in a tangled web of lies. He/she tells one lie to cover up their secret, and the lies continue one after the other to cover up the previous lies, all in a concerted effort to protect their hidden secret. It is a known fact that hidden secrets will eventually destroy the life of the deceiver and/or the lives of others involved. Deception, betrayal, and misrepresentation are components that eventually lead to a life of destruction. The believer who once held a firm stand for God now leads a life that is spiraling downhill from a believer to a deceiver and finally into a hypocrite.

The Original Greek translation of the word 'hypocrite' offers the illustration of a stage actor. A hypocrite is anyone who is simply putting on an act in order to deceive others. Actors usually wear costumes and pretend to be someone other than themselves. Instead of being who God called us to be many believers are living lives of deception and covering up the gift of the Holy Spirit with costumes in the form of lies, distrust, dishonesty, disloyalty, betrayal, and other characteristics dishonoring our Lord and Savior. Luke 8:17 (KJV) teaches that a hypocritical lifestyle cannot be concealed indefinitely. The Word of God says: "*For nothing is secret, that shall not be made manifest; neither any thing hid, that shall not be known and come abroad.*"

Our elders say it this way: what's done in the dark will definitely come to the light. Believers, it's time to pull off the mask and reveal our true identity. True believers of the Gospel cannot straddle the fence. We should love people enough to tell them the truth no matter the consequences. Instead, secrets are kept because the deceiver is ashamed, afraid of hurting others' feelings, or worried how others may react to their truth. Believers must take a stand before the world and declare Jesus as Lord over every aspect of our lives. Luke 16:13 comes with a warning that no servant can serve two masters: The heart will be either wholly taken up with God, or wholly engrossed with the world. The Message Bible makes it plain: "*If you're honest in small things, you'll be honest in big things; If you're a crook in small things, you'll be a crook in big things. If you're not honest in small jobs, who will put you in charge of the store? No worker can serve two bosses: He'll either hate the first and love the second or adore the first and despise the second. You can't serve both God and the Bank."* It's either black or white, up or down, in or out; it can't be one and the same. Believers cannot live secret lifestyles.

The choice to live a hypocritical lifestyle involves great risk: the risk of losing everything! Why risk damaging your reputation, damaging your career, breaking up families, and ruining the lives of many people, including your own. There is a way out before this hypocritical lifestyle unravels and you are exposed! The truth is, the secrets we keep are actually alive inside of us and they really want to be out of us. We give life to our secrets and they, too, want to live. Secrets want out of our minds and out of our bodies. Confession is the only way out!

Have you ever noticed that the majority of suspense movies or novels usually conclude where the criminal is caught because he or she talks too much and tells on himself? In a famous passage of "A Fragment of an Analysis of a Case of Hysteria," Freud writes, "He that has eyes to see and ears to hear may convince himself that no mortal can keep a secret. If his lips are silent, he chatters with his fingertips; betrayal oozes out of him at every pore." Our human nature does not possess the ability to keep secrets from others. Hypocrisy does not align with who we are. Our human nature confesses our secrets because we are not made to keep them, and deep down on the inside we do not want to. To live an authentic life before God we must confess our secrets.

The first step of confession is the hardest, but it is the most liberating thing that you will ever do. The first person to whom you must absolutely confess is yourself. You must come to grips with your errors and admit to yourself the secret things you have done or that you are currently doing. Be real with yourself, and if you are serious about change, then take the next step and remove yourself from the environment that condemns you. Trace the footsteps of your secret, and one step at a time eliminate the avenues of the tangled web you have created. Reclaim your identity by cutting off the things that have caused you to become a hypocrite. It will be painful at first, but your life depends upon your power to suck the life out of your secret. Your secret desires to live, and as long as you give life to it, it will!

The next step of confession will be just as difficult as the first one, but it must be done. You must tell your truth to another person. You need a reliable source to go to for confession. People are quick to judge others, and some people may reject you when your truth is revealed; but losing those people in exchange for your integrity and salvation is worth it. The truth is, people who genuinely have a love for you will love you no matter what and will be there to help you through the difficult times in your life. We all have that one person in our lives who we know that no matter what, they have our best interest at heart and will never do anything to hurt us or the people we love. It's important to share your secret with someone who will encourage you to live whole, and maintain courage and strength in the power of God.

Secret sharing involves a huge level of trust and one must be very selective with whom they decide to share their secrets. Be very selective and review the credentials of the person you are expecting to help you. Consider what this person has to add to your life, and also consider your level of expectation from them. Is the individual strong enough to handle your truth? Ask yourself, exactly what am I expecting this person to do to help me? Be very sure of the person you select, because the wrong person can hurt you. If you believe your truth is too much for the person you selected, you should consider seeking professional help from a therapist, counselor, pastor, religious adviser, or a twelve-step program. Our human nature loves gossip, and sharing your secrets with the wrong person will lead to the juicy details of your life being shared at the hair salon, PTA meetings, via text messages, plastered on Facebook, and even at the church house. People like gossip, and if you confide in the wrong person, you will become the headline story of the newsstands of others around you. From the very moment you say, "Can you keep a secret?" your life will never be the same again.

Gossip. It was gossip that led to one of the nation's most talked about scandals—the political scandal of the White House between former United States President, Bill Clinton, and twenty-two year old White House Intern, Monica Lewinsky. In 1995, Lewinsky, a graduate of Lewis & Clark College, was hired to work as an intern at the White House during Clinton's first term. While there, they both had an intimate relationship going on. Lewinsky confided the details of their secret affair to her friend and Defense Department co-worker, Linda Tripp, but had no idea that her so-called friend was secretly recording their telephone conversations.

Tripp recorded the conversations then shared the juicy gossip with others. The news of this extra-marital affair and the resulting investigation eventually led to the impeachment of President Clinton in 1998 by the U.S. House of Representatives and his subsequent acquittal on all impeachment charges of perjury and obstruction of justice in a 21-day Senate trial. For some reason, Ms. Lewinsky believed her fellow employee was someone she could trust, so she shared with her the hot and juicy details of her adulterous affair with the President of the United States. Their lives were forever changed because not only did Ms. Lewinsky share her secret with someone who could not be trusted, but she shared her secret with someone who could not provide anything to change her situation.

Think about it! What would her life look like had she shared her secret with God? I have no idea if Ms. Lewinsky ever prayed to God about her situation, but I do know that had she shared her secrets with God and not Linda Tripp, her life would have been very different. What would your life look like if you would talk to God about everything? Have you ever really considered the credentials of the person you share your secrets with? Even if the person you confide in never tells another soul, can this person really do anything to change your situation? We waste valuable time and unnecessary tears depending on others to do for us what only God can do. Jesus Christ is the only man who is able to change anything in our lives. God has a plan for our lives and His plan will come to pass.

This case alone is evidence that the only person you should confess your secret to is God. There are no hidden secrets with God. He knows all and He sees all. No matter how well you may think you have covered up your dirt, God already knows. And what I love about God is no matter what we have done His Word says if we confess our sins He will forgive us. Don't believe me; read it for yourself: *If we confess our sins, he is faithful and just to forgive us our sins, and to cleanse us from all unrighteousness* (I John 1:9, KJV). And I just love how the text reads in the God's Word Translation: *"God is faithful and reliable. If we confess our sins, he forgives them and cleanses us from everything we've done wrong.*

Thank You, Jesus! Others may turn their backs on us, but our God is faithful and we can rely on Him. Our level of expectation in our God is beyond what our minds can fathom. Jeremiah 33:3 (KJV) reminds us of what we should expect from our God when we call on Him: *"Call unto me, and I will answer thee, and show thee great and mighty things, which thou knowest not.* The Lord promises that when we seek Him, He will be there in ways that no man ever could.

As believers, we are encouraged to live by a level of expectation that the world will never understand. When faced with opposition and things that seem impossible, there is something on the inside of the believer that knows that our God is able to do exceedingly and abundantly above all. Our faith connects with the power of God, and we rest in the assurance that says "we know that all things work together for good to them that love God, to them who are the called according to his purpose." The b clause of Jeremiah 29:11 (KJV) reminds us that God will provide us with an expected end. The word 'expected' is translated in its original Hebrew language to mean: to wait, to tarry, to live for the thing I long for. The believer understands the essence of the cliche that we are so quick to quote, "He may not come when I want Him, but He is always on time!"

As a child, I can recall begging my father for a new bicycle. When I was growing up, we enjoyed playing outside and enjoyed making up our own games for entertainment. One of our favorite joys was bicycle riding. All the kids in our neighborhood would ride their bicycles up and down the streets in packs. After school, we would have daily racing events to see who had the fastest bike, and every afternoon my neighbor would win. I was convinced that my neighbor was winning because her father had purchased her a new bicycle that had twirly-twirly things hanging from the handlebars, and I was still riding my same old bicycle with no twirly things on my handlebars. I went to my father and told him I was tired of her beating me and I needed him to buy me a new bicycle with twirly-twirly things on the handlebars so that I could go fast. I can recall my father asking me if I really deserved a new bicycle. He said that in order to get it, there were some conditions that had to be met. My dad told me I had to keep my grades up, do my chores, and listen to my mother. Weeks went by and my father had not honored my request. I did everything my father instructed me to do, but still there was no bicycle.

I began to get extremely upset and went back to my father and reminded him of our conversation. I told him that he must have forgotten our conversation because he still had not purchased my bicycle and my neighbor was still beating me. My father assured me that he had not forgotten my request and he would make good on his promise. Again weeks went by and still no bicycle. We were on our way home from school one day. The school bus stopped in front of my neighbor's house and she said, "I'll be there to beat you in a few minutes." The bus pulled off and the driver made her usual right turn onto my street. I sat on the bus with my head hung low feeling disgusted and defeated. It wasn't until we pulled up to my house that I noticed my father standing on the driveway with a brand new bicycle just for me and it had twirly-twirly things on the handlebars. One of my friends asked me if I was going to race today and my father answered for me. He said, "Of course she is!" Dad told me to run inside, take off my school clothes, and put on my play clothes. I did just what my Dad told me then ran outside to try out my new bicycle.

It wasn't long before all the kids in my neighborhood were outside for our afternoon ride. I don't know who was the happiest—me or my father. Finally, my unbeaten neighbor showed up and challenged me to another race, and before I could say a word my father said, "Yeah, she's ready!" My father stood in the middle of the street counting us off, and I took off on my brand new bike. I can picture my pig tails and the twirly-twirly things racing down our street. After weeks of losing, I had finally won! I beat my neighbor! After weeks and weeks of begging and pleading, my father came through for me just like he promised. And my dad came through BIG! My bicycle had twirly-twirly things on the handlebars, little spokes that made this clicking sound on the wheels, and a basket on the front of it!

Later that night, I asked my father why he took so long to get me my bicycle. "I kept my grades up, I did all of my chores, and I listened to Mama just like you told me to. If you had purchased the bicycle weeks ago I could have been beaten the neighborhood champion already." My dad said, "Sweetie, you did exactly what I told you to do, and I have been trying to get your bicycle for months. I shopped the local stores, and no one had a pink bicycle with purple twirly-twirly things on the handlebars, and I wanted you to have what you asked me for." My father went on to say, "I could have bought you another bicycle, but you asked me for a pink bike with purple twirly-twirly things on the handlebars. The sales lady at one of the local department stores called and said a shipment had come in and she was holding the bicycle for me."

My dad said when he went to pick up the bicycle there was a box of bicycle baskets at the register and he told the sales lady to put one on my bicycle to make it extra special. He said the neighbor had twirly-twirly things on her bicycle, but she didn't have a basket on hers. He apologized because I had to wait, but told me to never give up on him. He reminded me that he had gotten me the baby doll that I begged for, the shoes I just couldn't live without, the board game I needed so badly, and even the convertible car that my doll just had to ride in for great style. He also said if he had done all those things for me before then I should have expected him to get me exactly what I asked for. Before going to bed, I had to tell my Daddy thank you because he not only fulfilled my request, but the basket on the front of my bicycle was over and beyond what I asked for.

As I sit back and think it over, I was happy and overjoyed but unsure why I expected anything less of my father. That's how our heavenly Father does. He always gives us His very best! Don't you know that God heard your request the very first time that you asked Him? A pink bike with purple twirly-twirly things on the handlebars, with spokes that made clicking sounds on the wheels, and a purple basket on the front was definitely a tall order. But there was nothing too big for my Daddy to handle. It may seem like nothing now, but I kept the secret of how painful it was for my friends to laugh at me for losing the bicycle race every single day.

I hid the pain I felt to have them make fun of me for losing race after race and having to listen to them talk about how old my bicycle had become. I made a decision to let go of my secret. I decided to tell my father and expected him to help me change my situation. I could have shared my secret with my sister, but she was in need of a new bicycle also. I could have shared my secret with my mother, but she would have consoled me and dried my tears after telling me she would tell my father. I decided to go to my daddy myself, and my father came through for me. Our heavenly Father is no different. Our Lord and Savior always gives us His very best! There are times in life when we wonder if God is listening, but do not worry; God heard your request the very first time you cried out to Him. Just like my earthly father came through for me, so did my heavenly Father.

On August 15, 2011, I suffered a ruptured brain

aneurysm that left my life dangling by a thread. Like most people I come in contact with, you may be wondering what a brain aneurysm is. A brain aneurysm is a bulging, weak area in the wall of an artery that supplies blood to the brain. The human body is an amazing anatomy that is controlled by our brains. Our brains communicate with every organ in our body. The Brain Aneurysm Foundation reports that ruptured brain aneurysms are fatal in about 40% of cases and of those who are fortunate to survive, about 66% will suffer some permanent deficit.

Just the idea of anything happening to your brain is very scary. Scary doesn't even describe how I felt. I spent an extensive amount of time in the hospital and, unfortunately, due to the damage to my brain, I have little to no memory of the events that occurred during my hospital stay. Listening to my family and friends recall this chapter of my journey always brings tears to my eyes. Over and over again, I have tried everything I can to bring back my memory. After visiting with my doctor, he informed me that I may never recall those memories. It is very possible that my short term memory may never return. However, it is very likely that my long term memory may return in time. Along with the other facts about my life that have changed, I am learning to live with it all.

There is one memory that I really wish I could forget. I do recall giving up on God. I had finally been released home after countless days in the hospital. It was hard enough returning to a home that I didn't even know belonged to me. In addition to that confusion were different nurses and therapists coming in and out all day long. It was so chaotic, but I was home and fighting to recover. Just when I assumed my hospital days were behind me, the doctor's office called for me to return again for a cerebral angiogram. A cerebral angiogram would provide a true picture of whether the stent assisted coil embolization to repair the ruptured aneurysm was holding or not. I immediately became fearful and thought the worst. I was readmitted and prepped for another surgery.

During my entire hospital stay, outside of me telling my family to get me out and demanding that they give me my cell phones, I never once whined, complained, or cried, even though by now I was tired of hospitals and really beginning to feel like I was going to die. I recall waking up in recovery with my husband seated on one side of the bed and my mother on the other. And I remember the nurse coming in to tell us that the doctor wanted to speak to us. At that moment, I knew in my heart that the news was bad, and I said to myself, "Well that's it; there is nothing else that can be done for me." Just days before the doctor telephoned my family to tell us that the last stent assisted coil embolization did not work and we would have to decide if we would try again or have the artery clipped.

Coiled or clipped? What's the difference? My thoughts were I'm damned if I do and damned if I don't. In my mind, I had had enough and I had lost all hope. The tough Arlicia had thrown in the towel and pulled out of the race. I laid in the recovery bed thinking of my children, family, and friends. I began to think of all the things in life that I wanted to do and hadn't yet accomplished. I thought of the places I dreamed of going and had not yet seen. I thought of missing the opportunity of seeing my children grow up and accomplish their dreams. I lay in bed and thought, "Wow! This is not fair!"

After the nurse left, my husband held one hand, my mother held my other hand and they began to pray. Their faith led them to pray, but my faith had begun to shift gears, and I could only think of how in the world the Lord could allow this to happen to me. I began to ask God, why? I wanted to know what it was that I had or had not done that would allow something so bad to happen to me. I heard them say that I may never walk and the uncertainty of what could occur in my life if we decided to clip the artery. I wanted to know from God, why?

The more they prayed, the madder I became. I wanted to yell and remind them, "Hey, have you guys taken a look at me? Do you see my bald head?" I wanted to say, "Didn't you hear the nurse say the doctor wants to talk to us. Stop wasting your time; it didn't work. It is what it is, and my time is up!" The truth is, I gave up on God! Finally, after what seemed to be hours later, the doctor came through the white curtains and before he could say a word, tears began to run down my face. The doctor walked in and asked me what was wrong. I said, "Well, what did you come to tell me?" He said he had news for us that he wanted to share himself. The doctor said, "Well, Arlicia, it worked!" I began to cry even harder. I looked at him and said, "So you didn't come to tell me I am going to die?" And he said, "Well, not if I have anything to do with it." He said, "We are going to keep praying, and I am going to keep working to keep you alive!" It appeared that everyone around me had more faith in God than I did.

In spite of my wavering faith, the Lord demonstrated His Power, His Provisions, and His Promises in my life. The odds were against me and probability didn't exist. Somewhere during my journey, faith and science connected and God did it. I had begun to give up on God, but little did I know that the Lord had prepared an expected end that my eyes could not see. During my journey, there were people praying and fasting all over the world for me, and I know without a shadow of a doubt that prayer is what has kept me alive. I have a vivid memory of receiving a telephone call of encouragement from a dear friend of mine, Dennis Jones, pastor of Gethsemane Missionary Baptist Church, in Houston, Texas. Pastor Jones encouraged me to remember Ephesians 3:20. He said, "Arlicia, no matter what the doctors may say, just remember that God is able to do exceedingly abundantly above all." Every time that we spoke either by telephone or via text message, Pastor Jones would say, "Just remember Ephesians 3:20." Pastor Jones was so right.

I couldn't see it at that moment, but as I consider all that God has done in my life, God has been true to His Word. Here, Paul encourages us in the faith with these words: *Now unto him that is able to do exceeding abundantly above all that we ask or think, according to the power that worketh in us.*

I love the Message Bible Translation of the text: *God can do anything, you know—far more than you could ever imagine or guess or request in your wildest dreams! He does it not by pushing us around but by working within us, his Spirit deeply and gently within us. Glory to God in the church! Glory to God in the Messiah, in Jesus! Glory down all the generations! Glory through all millennia! Oh, yes!*

When I wanted a new bicycle I went to my daddy, and not only did he give me what I asked for, but he gave me more than I imagined. I wanted a pink bicycle with purple twirly-twirly things on the handlebars, and he gave me a pink bicycle with purple twirly-twirly things on the handlebars, clicking sounding things on the spokes, and a purple basket on the front. This lesson alone should have reminded me never to give up on my heavenly Father. Although I couldn't understand, although I couldn't see it, and even though it didn't make sense, I should have exercised the same faith in my heavenly Father, expecting Him to heal my body.

The Lord allowed an experimental surgery to repair my ruptured brain aneurysm that human doctors didn't even know would work. The Lord repaired my rupture, gave me the activity of my limbs, restored my sight, restored my speech, and gave me the right frame of mind. My God has proven that He is able. The Lord answered my prayers and gave me exceeding abundantly above all that my mind could ever imagine. Our God is an ABLE God! With every breath inside of my body, I want to tell the world what God has done for me. Victoria isn't the only sister with a secret; I have one too! Let me share my secret with you.

When a brain aneurysm ruptures, the result is called

a subarachnoid hemorrhage. Depending on the severity of the hemorrhage, brain damage or death may result. The most common location for brain aneurysms is in the network of blood vessels at the base of the brain called the Circle of Willis. My aneurysm was even more rare because it was located on the right side of my brain. It was extremely difficult to get to due to its size and location. Although rare in nature, neurosurgeons at the University of Texas Medical School - Memorial Hermann Hospital in Houston, Texas, were prepared for cases of this nature. Little did anyone know that on August 15th, 2011, there would be not one, but two patients, life-flighted, both with this rare aneurysm located on the right side of the brain on the same night. Yes, I was one of the two.

The neurosurgeons had been studying and preparing for a case like this, and on that night fate would have it that two patients arrived both bleeding on the brain and both on the brink of death. The surgical procedure that saved my life was experimental. My family was asked to allow me to participate in a Humanitarian Use Device (HUD) project called "Cordis Enterprise Vascular Reconstruction Device and Delivery System – Humanitarian Use Device" conducted by Dr. Peng Roc Chen and his research staff at the University of Texas Health Science Center Houston. A Humanitarian Use Device is a device that is "intended to benefit patients in the treatment and diagnosis of diseases or conditions that affect fewer than 4000 individuals in the United States." This HUD was FDA approved but experimental because there were too few patients with this type of aneurysm to allow for traditional clinical trial testing to be performed in a timely manner.

It was later reported to my family that at the time of my rupture the HUD performed by this research team had been performed on five patients and of *the five patients, two of them died and two remained in a vegetative state AND I, me, Arlicia Renee Beverly-Albert, has been the ONLY ONE who God has favored to walk and tell it!* I do not know if the other patient who arrived that night died or remains in a vegetative state, but what I do know is that the Lord favored my life beyond my wildest dreams. Things did not have to go that way, BUT GOD! GOD DID IT!

I wanted to know why the Lord allowed this to happen, and the Lord whispered in my ear and again told me, *For I know the thoughts that I think toward you, saith the Lord, thoughts of peace, and not of evil, to give you an expected end.* My life may not be going the way I planned it, but it is going EXACTLY the way GOD planned it. Little did I know that my God had planned to use my life to demonstrate to the world that He is an able God for *now unto him that is able to do exceeding abundantly above all that we ask or think, according to the power that worketh in us.*

The Message Bible's translation of these two Scriptures will blow your mind. Check it out: *I'll show up and take care of you as I promised and bring you back home. I know what I'm doing. I have it all planned out — plans to take care of you, not abandon you, plans to give you the future you hope for. God can do anything, you know — far more than you could ever imagine or guess or request in your wildest dreams!*

The Lord told me that He allowed it to happen because He knew I would not keep what He has done for me a secret. The Lord knew I had a big mouth, and I would tell it all. The Lord knew if He blew my mind and performed a miracle in my life that I would become a mouthpiece for Him telling the world that without a doubt my life proves that GOD still works miracles! God did it! Don't give up on God because He surely won't give up on you. He's able! No matter what you need from God, the shout of the day is: "It's no secret what my God can do. What He's done for others He will do for you!"

God Will Do it!

What Are You Expecting from God?
Take a moment and make note of exactly what you

are expecting God to do in your life.

_____

_____

_____

_____

_____

_____

_____

Secrets from our Savior

"Believe me: I am in my Father and my Father is in me. If you can't believe that, believe what you see—these works. The person who trusts me will not only do what I'm doing but even greater things, because I, on my way to the Father, am giving you the same work to do that I've been doing. You can count on it. From now on, whatever you request along the lines of who I am and what I am doing, I'll do it. That's how the Father will be seen for who he is in the Son. I mean it. Whatever you request in this way, I'll do."
--John 14:11-14, MSG

"This is God's Message, the God who made earth, made it livable and lasting, known everywhere as God: 'Call to me and I will answer you. I'll tell you marvelous and wondrous things that you could never figure out on your own.'" --Jeremiah 33:2-3, MSG

"And now I have it all—and keep getting more! The gifts

you sent with Epaphroditus were more than enough, like a sweet-smelling sacrifice roasting on the altar, filling the air with fragrance, pleasing God no end. You can be sure that God will take care of everything you need, his generosity exceeding even yours in the glory that pours from Jesus. Our God and Father abounds in glory that just pours out into eternity. Yes." --Philippians 4:18-20, MSG

"God can do anything, you know—far more than you could ever imagine or guess or request in your wildest dreams! He does it not by pushing us around but by working within us, his Spirit deeply and gently within us. Glory to God in the church! Glory to God in the Messiah, in Jesus! Glory down all the generations! Glory through all millennia! Oh, yes!" --Ephesians 3:20-21, MSG

Sisters' Authority
Pray This Prayer of Expectation:

Lord, thank You for the promises I find in Your Word. Lord, from the book of Genesis to the book of Revelation, Your Word promises to give me an expected end. Your Word declares that: You will "Give me the desires of my heart"; You will "make my enemies my footstool"; You will "go before me and make every crooked path straight"; Your Word would not return unto You void; It shall accomplish that which You please; and It shall prosper in the thing whereto You send It. You promise to "pour me out a blessing that I will not have room enough to receive"; that "no good thing would you withhold from me"; that no weapon formed against me would prosper; and that I can ask anything in Your name and You would do it." Lord, thank You for Your promises. Master, I ask that You give me the strength to see Your hands at work in my life even when things do not go as I have planned. Give me the strength to seek the plan that You have for my life, strength to leap over the hurdles, to step out of the pit holes, to wipe the tears from my eyes, to crawl out of the valley, to dust off the spirit of defeat, and to buckle my seat belt as You propel me into my destiny. Lord, I am grateful Your plan never fails. I pray this prayer in faith, thankful that I have Your Word, I know Your Word, and I expect Your Word to be honored in my life. In Jesus' Name I Pray! Amen!

Sisters' Declarations

Declarations help us *"call those things that are not as though they are."* - Romans 4:17b

We call Abraham "father" not because he got God's attention by living like a saint, but because God made something out of Abraham when he was a nobody. Isn't that what we've always read in Scripture, God saying to Abraham, "I set you up as father of many peoples"? Abraham was first named "father" and then became a father because he dared to trust God to do what only God

could do: raise the dead to life, with a word make something
out of nothing. When everything was hopeless, Abraham
believed anyway, deciding to live not on the basis of what
he saw he couldn't do but on what God said he would do.
And so he was made father of a multitude of peoples. God
himself said to him, "You're going to have a big family,
Abraham!" --Romans 4:17-18, MSG.

No matter what may be seen by the physical eye, our faith and trust in God speaks life even when it still looks dead. Our God has a way of bringing life to dead places, people, nations, and situations. The essence of faith is to believe before we see, not to see to believe. By declaring things alive that look dead, we become like God in *"calling those things that are not as though they are."*

The Word of God provides a solution to every situation that you will face in life. No matter the situations that occur, make a decision to declare today to seek God and hold fast to His promises. Make a decision that says: Today, I declare that I will pray to my Heavenly Father and trust the plan that He has purposed and willed for my life. To avoid having my past collide with my present, I have made the decision to speak victory over my life.

Victory Declaration

I declare that God has a great plan for my life. In

every situation, I will seek God and wait on Him. God will show up and take care of everything in my life just as He promised. And even though I may not always understand how, God will work out every detail to my advantage. He will be faithful to His promise and never leave me stranded. I expect Him to reveal His plan for my life in His own time, and it will be right on time. This is my declaration.

My Ephesians 3:20 Declaration

I declare Ephesians 3:20 over my life. I know that my God is ABLE to do anything. The favor of God will bless me far more than what I could ever dream or imagine. I am not intimidated by the enemy and the false picture he tries to portray before me. I have placed my trust in God, and His blessings will flood my life. I will not give up on my dreams. I will pray bold prayers and expect big things in return. I am surrounded by God's favor, and I will walk in the favor of my personal Ephesians 3:20. This is my declaration.

Let the enemy hear you speak Ephesians 3:20 ALOUD

God can do anything, you know—far more than you could ever imagine or guess or request in your wildest dreams! He does it not by pushing us around but by working His Spirit deeply and gently within us. Glory to God in the church! Glory to God in the Messiah, in Jesus! Glory down all the generations! Glory through all millennia! Oh, yes! (Ephesians 3:20-21, MSG)

Glory to God for My Ephesians 3:20!
After reading this publication, I declare today that my life will never be the same again. Victory is mine! Victoria isn't the only sister with a secret. I know the secret, I have the secret, and the secret will be revealed in my life for my God is ABLE! Today I fully embrace MYE320.

Afterword

When I wrote and published "This One Is For Us" through my personal blog on April 22, 2013, I had no idea that it would find its way to Capitol Hill in Washington, D.C., where a copy of it landed in the hands of Mrs. Arlicia Albert, who would then connect to me via Facebook and ask me to write an afterword for this book. However, that is just a prime example of the ways in which God works. As Proverbs 19:21 reads, "Many are the plans in a person's heart, but it is the Lord's purpose that prevails." Of course, I hadn't planned to experience a hemorrhagic stroke due to a ruptured brain aneurysm at the age of 24, nor did I plan to begin writing about my journey and have my struggles reach across the oceans and impact others who have been through this journey. When I first came home after nearly half a month in the hospital, I had zero intentions of even talking about what had happened to me, and I didn't want to share it at large. I was in a state of disbelief and immense hurt. I had just turned 24 two months and two days before "my brain exploded," and I had plenty of questions, with very few answers. Writing has always been a passion of mine and a gift given to me straight from the Lord. Had the same stroke (right temporal lobe) occurred on the left side of my brain, I probably wouldn't be able to write these words today. Through my trials and the struggle, I have been truly blessed. What I could have easily used for momentum to live a bitter, unhappy, broken-spirited life, the Lord has used to lift me higher. I didn't want to hear it then, but my mother and many others who prayed over me were right when they said I would come out "a better Robin."

So many times in life, we make plans and goals for ourselves or we allow others to, and we are so determined to meet those goals. Our vision is narrow and our drive is relentless. We must reach this goal by this time, or else our life is considered nothing to us. Life doesn't always go the ways we plan, but we have to trust the timing of our lives and walk our designated paths. The trouble comes when we are so set on our ideals that we forget there is a Creator whose plan for us is greater. We may not understand His plan or even agree with it, but we have to accept that He knows more than we do and allow Him to direct our paths. Choosing to trust Him is also choosing to live in faith, and sometimes that means resigning so much of what you have for you, to accept and believe that what He has for you is greater. This is no easy task, but if you trust that He'll hold true to His promises, you will find that He will bless your life with so much greater, just as Ephesians 3:20 reads.

Arlicia has been a great joy to my life in the short time we've come to know each other, and I am grateful for another survivor friend who encouraged her to contact me on Facebook, which is how we began this survivor sister friendship. It just so happens that we both live in Texas, as well. I would call it a coincidence, but I serve a God, who always has a plan. What looks like a coincidence to us is often just another piece of the grand puzzle He has made of each of our lives. I have no doubts that for some reason, He conjoined our paths. I find it ironically funny that had I never began my blog to detail my setbacks and successes, I would never have "met" Arlicia or any of the survivors who I have now adopted into my survivor friend family. Arlicia and I have shared several stories filled with laughter, hopes, frustrations, and encouragement to keep fighting through. To think I didn't want to ever speak a word of what I went through! We are strong, we serve a mighty God, who is able, even when we feel that we are not able. I know for a fact that I continue to give Him the praise, whether it is through a storm or the sun is shining down on me.

I hope that you, like I have, find something in this book that reaches out to you and touches your soul. I honestly believe that there is a brightness to this book that can shed a little light upon anyone's path. That is why we are called here, anyway. It is not enough to speak of the light; we must become the light. As I mentioned in the beginning, I had never planned on writing about my journey, but it has now become one of the most instrumental parts of my recovery, as it has allowed me access to a world I had never known before. It was not my plan, but His, and I am grateful for that. When I felt as though I was going through a desert, never to see an oasis again, God slowly drew me out of myself, allowing me to connect with others, and He has been restoring me into a better me, every day. Truly as Isaiah 58:11 reads, "The Lord will guide you always; He will satisfy your needs in a sunscorched land and will strengthen your frame. You will be like a well-watered garden, like a spring whose waters never fail." He has held true to His promise to me. I thank Him every day for the opportunities given to me as a result of my struggle and I praise Him for the many successes, relationships, and blessings He has bestowed upon me. Arlicia, thank you for extending this great opportunity to me, my survivor sister! To you, and any readers of this book, always remember to keep the faith and keep the fight!

Brain Aneurysm Survivor
Robin J. Reid
"This One Is For Us"

Who is Victoria?

Here's The Answer You Have All Been Waiting For...

Yes, Victoria is a real person! But no, she is no one person. Victoria represents the lives of so many women that I have come in contact with. It is my sincere prayer that after reading this publication at some point you were able to see yourself in the life of Victoria. Now, I pray that you never encounter a Pimp dressed up like a Leprechaun or ever come close to a sexual encounter with your father, however; it is my prayer that you have a strong spiritual foundation.

Perhaps you have read this publication yet you have not accepted Jesus Christ as your Lord and Savior. Please know that God loves you, and he desires to have a personal relationship with you through Jesus, His Son. This journey called LIFE is real and making decisions is tough but accepting Jesus Christ into your life will prove to be the best decision ever made.

Secret To Spiritual Freedom

I. Admit you are a sinner.

No one ever likes to admit it but, "we all have sinned and come short of the glory of God" (Romans 3:23). We sin by things we do, choices we make, attitudes we display, the private thoughts we entertain and by just down right refusing to do better when we know better. The truth is, we are all sinners.

II. Understand that as a sinner, you deserve death.

A life of sin has it's consequences. "For the wages of sin is death" (Romans 6:23a). Our sins demand punishment and we should be justly punished for our choices of sin. Our lying lips, deceitful tongue, and perverted actions deserve the punishment of death and separation from God. But, because of His great love, God sent His only Son Jesus to die for our sins.

III. Believe Jesus Christ died on the cross to save you from sin and death.

Because of our sins, we deserve death. "But the gift of God is eternal life through Jesus Christ our Lord" (Romans 6:23b). Romans 5:8 declares, "But God demonstrates His own love toward us, in that while we were still sinners, Christ died for us. " If you have ever wondered what does love look like? Love looks like Jesus dying on the cross just for me. Now, that's love!

IV. Repent by turning from your old life of sin to a new life in Christ.

Confess that you are a sinner and leave the life of sin behind. Make a turn toward Christ and follow Jesus. Romans 10:9-10, "That if thou shalt confess with thy mouth the Lord Jesus, and shalt believe in thine heart that God hath raised him from the dead, thou shalt be saved. For with the heart man believeth unto righteousness; and with the mouth confession is made unto salvation". Because of Jesus' death on our behalf, all we have to do is believe in Him, trusting His death as the payment for our sins - and we will be saved! Romans 10:13 says it again, "for everyone who calls on the name of the Lord will be saved." Jesus died to pay the penalty for our sins and rescue us from eternal death.

V. Receive, through faith in Jesus Christ, his free gift of salvation.

Receive the gift of salvation! Romans 5:1 has this wonderful message, "Therefore, since we have been justified through faith, we have peace with God through our Lord Jesus Christ." Through Jesus Christ, we can have a relationship of peace with God. Romans 8:1 teaches us, "Therefore, there is now no condemnation for those who are in Christ Jesus." Because of Jesus' death on our behalf, we will never be condemned for our sins. We have this precious promise of God from Romans 8:38-39, "For I am convinced that neither death nor life, neither angels nor demons, neither the present nor the future, nor any powers, neither height nor depth, nor anything else in all creation, will be able to separate us from the love of God that is in Christ Jesus our Lord." NOTHING will keep me from my Savior!

Please pray this prayer of salvation:

Lord, thank you for dying on the cross for me. If it had not been for your love, I don't know where I would be. Lord I am a sinner and I do not deserve your blessings but because of your love, I am given the blessing of another chance. Jesus, come into my life, take control of my life, forgive my sins and save me. I am now placing my trust in You alone for my

salvation, and I accept your free gift of eternal life."
If you've prayed this prayer of salvation with true
conviction and heart, you are now a follower of Jesus.
Welcome to the Family of God!

www.ingramcontent.com/pod-product-compliance
Lightning Source LLC
LaVergne TN
LVHW051119080426
835510LV00018B/2129